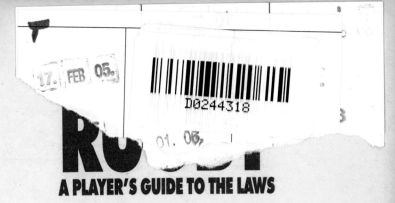

WO

A PLAYER'S GUIDE TO THE LAWS

Derek Robinson was born in 1932. After National Service in the RAF (spent claustrophobically in underground ops rooms) he went up to Cambridge on a State Scholarship and read History. He planned to be a journalist but the money looked grim so he went into advertising instead – five years in London, six in New York, working on everything from bulldozers and whisky to oil companies and *The Wall Street Journal*. In 1967 he gave it all up and lived in Portugal for a year, then returned via the Channel Islands to England where he and his American wife now live. He has written eight novels, of which the best known are *Goshawk Squadron* and *Piece of Cake*, plus books on squash and rugby and a best-selling guide to West Country dialect called *Krek Waiter's Peak Bristle*. He was the writer in the Rugby Football Union team that produced *The Laws in Plain English* for the International Rugby Football Board. He also broadcasts occasionally.

RUGBY

A PLAYER'S GUIDE TO THE LAWS

DEREK ROBINSON

CollinsWillow
An Imprint of HarperCollinsPublishers

For their great help in the preparation of this book,
my thanks to (in alphabetical order):
R.A.B. (Jim) Crowe, Past President of the London Society of
Rugby Football Union Referees,
Peter Hughes, Past Chairman RFU Laws Sub-Committee
and Don Rutherford, Technical Director, RFU

Any errors, inaccuracies or blemishes are
down to me and not to them

This book covers all changes to the Laws of Rugby
up to and including those made in 1998

First edition published in 1995 by
CollinsWillow
an imprint of HarperCollins*Publishers*
London

Revised edition 1998

© Derek Robinson 1995, 1996, 1998

ISBN 0 00 218863 5
ISBN (Aus/NZ edition) 0 00 218886 4

Printed and bound in Great Britain by
Caledonian International Book Manufacturer

Contents

Foreword

Some people think that referees like me, lucky enough to be on the international panel, do nothing but take big matches in exotic countries. If only!

There's no denying we see the world. So far I've had the privilege of refereeing 25 international matches, and rugby has taken me to many nations – from Australia to Argentina, from Italy to the USA, and from France to South Africa, where I was fortunate enough to take the 1995 World Cup Final.

Nevertheless, I still get plenty of opportunity to referee at the game's grass roots – schoolboy, colts, student, junior clubs – as well as league and cup games.

And one thing stands out in all of them – one consistent factor. *Any team that doesn't understand the laws of the game is in trouble.* Before you can start to win, you must know what's allowed and what's not. That's as true in a World Cup Final as it is in a 3rd XV run-around.

This book is the answer to many players' questions.

What I especially like about it is its wit and imagination. It turns the official law-book inside-out and shows not only how each law works but also why it's needed and what difference it makes to the game. That's a very user-friendly approach. With seventy excellent pictures, this is definitely my kind of book. It should be yours, too.

Ed Morrison

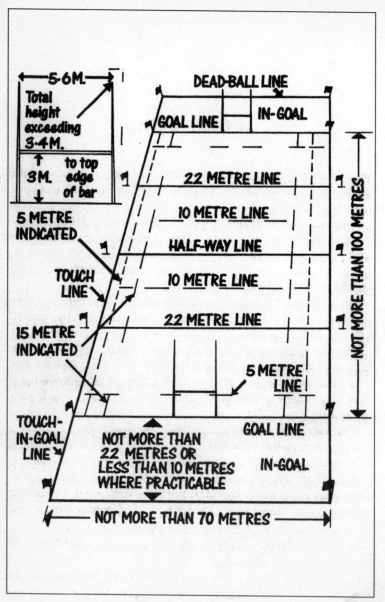

Plan of the playing area.

Introduction

There is no secret about how to play rugby, any more than there is a secret about how to play basketball, tennis, or stud poker. The laws of the game are written down for all to see. There may be many secrets about how to *win*, but there is no secret about how to play.

Moreover, it's pretty obvious that a player should learn how to play a game before he starts thinking about how to win. Any poker player who got into a game without knowing whether a full house beats a flush, or vice versa, would have a pretty unhappy time of it.

Yet it is a fact that tens of thousands of rugby players do not fully understand the laws of their game. What's more, these players have given up hope of ever knowing all the laws. They were never properly taught them when they began playing and they don't intend to start learning them now.

As a result, tens of thousands of players are playing well below their true capacity. Simply because they don't completely understand what is allowed and what is prohibited, they can never be sure that they are making the most of the first, and steering clear of the second.

This has nothing to do with a player's physical fitness, experience, or natural ability. It makes no difference whether a man is playing for a first-class club or his local pub XV – either he understands a particular law, or he doesn't. And if he doesn't, then he must be handicapped when playing against opponents who do, even if they're less fit, less experienced, or less gifted than he is. That, too, is pretty obvious.

You may think that ignorance is ignorance. Life isn't as simple as that. In rugby, there's active ignorance, passive ignorance, and cock-eyed ignorance.

Take the law of offside. A player who doesn't realise that he is in an offside position is liable to charge into the game and risk giving away a penalty kick. On the other hand, if he is not sure whether he's *on*side, he may do nothing at all. This is the result of *active* ignorance, and that's exactly what the other team likes to see.

It gets worse. Suppose he's penalised for offside play. He still doesn't know exactly what he did wrong. All he knows is the enemy is taking a pot at goal and it's his fault.

So in future he hangs back, afraid of repeating the mistake – a mistake which he can't really describe, even to himself.

Today, when kickers can slot penalties from any part of their opponents' half, indescribable mistakes are something no team can afford.

Then there's the player who doesn't take all his chances because he doesn't fully understand the laws. Often this has nothing to do with the referee. The referee applies the laws that lay down what players must or must not do. There are plenty of laws that tell the player what he *may* do, if he wants to. If he doesn't grab his chance, the game won't break down; but a good opportunity will slip away. This is the effect of *passive* ignorance – ignorance of the freedom which the laws allow.

A good example is the advantage law. A player who doesn't know how it works is not ready to seize on his opponents' mistakes and benefit from them. His failure is not that he's breaking the laws, but that he isn't getting the most out of them.

Finally, there's the player who has picked up a lot of half-baked half-truths, usually from friends who gave up playing fifteen years ago. This is *cock-eyed* ignorance.

A good example is the belief that it is always illegal for a player on the ground to pass the ball. This happens, and an opponent shouts: 'Passing off the ground, ref!' When the ref ignores him, he feels robbed. He loses heart. His cock-eyed ideas may not be illegal, but they certainly weaken his game. (If you're still not happy about passing off the ground, see Chapter 3. There *are* some occasions when it's *not* legal.)

The fact that so many players are resigned to going through their playing careers without fully understanding what they're doing is extraordinary. And yet it's true. In no other sport are the players so vague about the laws of the game. Yet the laws of rugby are not much more difficult than those of other games. Indeed, rugby is based on one very simple idea; the idea that each player should be as free as possible to get the ball and help his side score with it.

That obviously cuts out any interference with a player who hasn't got the ball. It lets everybody concentrate on the man who *has* got it. And it means that any number of players may handle, kick or pass the ball, one after another, keeping the game going continuously.

When you know the basic principles behind rugby, the laws become quite straightforward. Rugby is meant to be fast-moving and continuous, with as few stoppages as possible, so the laws are against things like deliberately lying on the ball, or refusing to let go of it when you're tackled. The aim is *positive* – to keep the game going and the ball moving, and let everyone get on with it. That's why there are clear-cut laws against foul play, such as obstruction or dangerous play.

The idea behind scrums and line-outs is simple: to restart the game, quickly and fairly, once it's stopped.

The purpose of the offside law is to keep each team more or less intact. It also gives a team space to play the ball when they've won it fairly. A man is offside when he's in front of a player on his own team who has the ball or who last played it, and for the moment he's out of the game. It's as simple as that. Without offside the game would become so scattered and confused that, like the retreat from Moscow, you couldn't see the action for the players. Offside makes the difference between an all-for-one and a free-for-all.

The law against throwing the ball forward makes sense once you understand offside. If you give a forward pass, the man who takes it must be in front of you. And if you mustn't throw it forward, you obviously shouldn't *knock* it forward either; hence the law against the knock-on.

These laws are both simple and useful. If you abolished offside, allowed forward passes and ignored knock-ons, the result wouldn't be better rugby; it would be a kind of sloppy handball.

The need for laws about scoring, kicking and the in-goal (where scoring takes place) is pretty obvious. Finally, there is the advantage law, which can trump nearly all the rest. This simply allows the referee to let play continue when one team breaks a law and their opponents take advantage of this. The advantage law covers ninety-nine per cent of all rugby.

True rugby can be played only if the players know the laws and honestly try to follow them. Accidentally breaking the law is bad luck; deliberately doing so is trying to distort the whole shape of the game. It's cheating in its most childish form because in the long run the player is only cheating himself. It's the players who benefit from the laws so it's up to the players to apply them.

That's why there's only one referee for thirty players. If everyone uses the laws and doesn't abuse them, one referee is all you need.

The better you know the laws, the more you'll enjoy the game. If the French, Italians, Poles, Japanese, Rumanians, Portuguese, Fijians and God-knows-who-else can master them, so can you. There is no secret about rugby, but before you start thinking about how to win games, you should make sure you know what the game itself is all about. Winning rugby starts here.

1
Offside in open play

Not at scrums, rucks, mauls or line-outs

'More players have nervous breakdowns trying to understand the offside law,' a research expert recently reported, 'than get kicked to death by green canaries.'

Which is a pity, because offside is basically simple. In open play, you are offside when you are in front of a player of your own team who has the ball, or who last played it. ('In front of' means 'nearer your opponents' dead-ball line'.) And you must not take part in the game in any way until you become onside again.

This means much more than not touching the ball or the opponent who has the ball. It means that when you are offside because a team-mate behind you has kicked the ball ahead of you, then you must not even move towards the ball. Move *back or sideways*, if you wish, but not towards the ball or the enemy waiting to play the ball. He may be fifty yards away. Tough luck. You can't take a step in his direction until you've been put onside. You can't do anything at all to influence the course of the game except breathe in and out. Temporarily, you are on ice.

What's more, if you are offside and you are near where the ball is about to land, you must beat it fast, until you're at least ten metres away. More on that later.

Take comfort. There is nothing to be ashamed, disgusted or suicidal about in being offside. Everybody is offside at some time or other. You get into trouble only when you try to take part in the game before you have been put properly onside.

Two kinds of offside

The ball is behind you

Firstly, there's offside because a team-mate behind you has the ball or has just passed it or dropped it. The point is he touched it last and it's still behind you. You're in an offside position but you can go where you like, provided you don't obstruct an opponent. Also, you must not play the ball if it comes your way. For instance, if a team-mate behind you knocks-on in your direction, you'd better leave the ball alone, or you'll be in trouble. Even if an opponent grabs it, you can't immediately grab him. You're still offside and out of the game until you've been put onside.

There's no penalty, though, for being in an offside position as

Offside when in front of the ball. A player is offside when he's in front of a team-mate who has the ball. In this situation, the offside player is free to go anywhere, provided he doesn't interfere with play by obstructing an opponent. Starbursts indicate offside players.

Offside when behind the ball. A player is offside when a team-mate behind him has kicked the ball ahead of him. In this situation, the offside player must not move towards the ball. He must stand still or move back, until he's put onside. Starbursts indicate offside players.

long as you don't get involved in play. If the ball's behind you, you're certainly not obliged to stand still.

The ball is in front of you

Second, there's offside because a team-mate behind you has kicked the ball and put it in front of you. This is the situation already described, where you must not move towards the ball or your opponents who are waiting to play the ball. Even if they don't catch the kick, even if they let it bounce, the offside player must not go forwards.

The kick may be huge. The nearest opponent may be half the field away. It makes no difference. Anyone who is offside when a team-mate boots the ball over his head must stand still (or move backwards) until he's been put onside. If he takes a step forward, he may be penalised.

What good does offside do?

It is not hard to see the reason for the offside law, once you see the mess we'd be in without it. If players could station themselves anywhere in the field, no matter where play was, you would have some of them camping permanently on their opponents' goal-line, just waiting for the ball to be booted their way. Players would be scattered everywhere, and both sides would constantly kick ahead in the hope of reaching someone and getting an easy score. Rugby would be basketball or, worse still, soccer.

As it is, offside does not paralyse a player; it just keeps him quiet (off-the-side) until he has been put onside and has thus rejoined the team (on-the-side). Offside in French is *hors-jeu* – out of the game. That says everything.

That justifies most offside. But what about the situation where an offside player can't even take a step forward, just because a team-mate behind him has kicked ahead? The kicker may be in one 22, and the catcher in the other. That's a big gap. What's the harm in letting an offside player close the gap by a few paces?

Go back a few years. Teams (especially in Australia) worked out a way to stifle an enemy attack. The full-back put in a long, high kick. While the ball was in the air, the rest of his team raced after it.

As the laws stood then, they were all offside but not liable to penalty because they took care to stop when they were at least ten metres from the catcher. He caught the ball, looked up and saw a line of opponents spread across the field, so close he could see the whites of their eyes. Attacking prospects: poor. So he booted the ball back from where it came, hotly pursued by *his* team. And so on. It was aerial ping-pong. It was not rugby. The lawmakers changed the law. 'You want to kick possession away?' they said. 'Fine. But only your onside players can chase it. The others are out of the game, until they're put onside.'

Being in front of the ball does not make you offside

You're only offside if you're *in front of a team-mate who has the ball*, or who last played it. (This is in open play, remember.) So if your opponents have the ball you can be well in front of it – nearer their goal line – and you're not offside. Sometimes this *looks* wrong. Suppose Reds are playing Blues. A Red attack breaks down. Blues come away with the ball, passing and running and gaining ground. A Red attacker (ex-attacker) chases after them. He is, of course, in front of the ball; that is, nearer Blues' goal line. Blues drop a pass. The Red player arrives and grabs it. The crowd howls: *Offside!* They're mistaken. Who last played the ball? His opponents did. And that's what matters.

Readers write

T.D. of Leatherhead writes: You can't tell me that refs apply the offside law as strictly as you make out. I'm talking about the situation where a player kicks ahead, over the top of his team, and you say they have to stand still.

D.R. Or move back.

T.D. And if one of them so much as takes half a pace forward, he gets penalised? I don't believe it. Besides, there's up to fourteen offside players. The ref can't watch them all, can he?

D.R. You'd be surprised how much a good referee can see. Still, you have a point. But remember, advantage may apply. What matters is whether or not an offside player moving forward is liable to influence play. For instance, if he's near the right-hand touch line while his opponents are successfully attacking down the left, the ref may ignore him and let them carry on enjoying themselves.

* * *

R.S.J. of Northampton writes: Changing the law of offside in open play hasn't worked. You still get the full-backs kicking the ball from 22 to 22, each hoping the other will knock-on. It's boring.

D.R. Don't tell me. Tell them. There's nothing in the law-book that forces teams to play good rugby.

2
Onside in open play
The ten-metre law • Also penalties

1 TEAM-MATE WITH BALL RUNS AHEAD

2 OFF-SIDE PLAYER RUNS BEHIND BALL CARRIER

3 & 4 TEAM-MATE KICKS, RUNS AHEAD OR ANOTHER ON--SIDE TEAM-MATE RUNS AHEAD.

If you are not in front of a team-mate who has the ball, or who last played the ball, you are onside. ('In front' means 'nearer your opponents' dead-ball line'.) Onside means you are not offside, so you can take part in the game.

I'm still talking about open play. Scrums, rucks, mauls and line-outs are different.

When you're offside, there are *seven* ways of getting yourself put onside.

Four depend on what your team does. *Three* depend on what your opponents do.

Put onside by your own team

1. When a team-mate, carrying the ball, runs in front of you, he puts you onside.
2. When a team-mate who kicked the ball when he was behind you, now runs in front of you, he puts you onside.
3. When any other team-mate who was onside when the ball was kicked, now runs in front of you, he puts you onside.
4. When you run behind any one of these team-mates, he puts you onside.

Put onside by your opponents
(but not under the Ten-Metre Law)

In this situation, you're in front of a team-mate who has kicked ahead. An opponent gets possession of the ball (he catches it or picks it up), or he intentionally touches it.

1. When an opponent runs 5 metres with the ball, he puts you onside.
2. When an opponent plays the ball – kicks it or passes it or just plain drops it – he puts you onside.
3. When an opponent intentionally touches the ball but doesn't catch it, he puts you onside.

(Opposite) Put onside by your team: 4 ways. In general play, an offside player is put onside when (1) the ball-carrier runs in front of him, or (2) he runs behind the ball-carrier, or (3) a team-mate kicks ahead and runs in front of him, or (4) any other team-mate who was onside when the ball was kicked runs in front of him.

Put onside by an opponent: 3 ways. In general play, an offside player is put onside when an opponent (1) runs 5 metres with the ball, or (2) kicks or passes it, or (3) intentionally touches it but doesn't catch it. (None of this applies to an offside player within 10 metres of where the ball lands.)

Onside balances offside

The laws try to discourage you from getting offside by making you do a little penance before they let you back into the game. You have to return to your team, or wait until your team (in the shape of an onside player) comes up and joins you. Note that, in a kick-ahead situation, you can be put onside by any other player on your team who was onside when the ball was kicked. So even if the kicker is brought down as he makes his kick, and is unable to follow it up, any player level with him or behind him can run forward and put his team-mates onside.

In short, you can be put onside by any player who is himself onside when the ball is kicked.

But *until* you're put onside, you must keep out of the game and give your opponents room for one free go – a chance to start something without fear of interruption from you. Only when one of them has run five metres with the ball, or passed it, or kicked it, or done *something*, can you come out of your trance and join in the action again.

And sometimes you cannot even do that, as we shall now reveal.

The Ten-Metre Offside Law

If you're offside and less than ten metres from an opponent who is waiting to catch the ball, there's only one thing to do: get the hell out of it. This situation usually arises when a team-mate behind you kicks the ball ahead, and an opponent is waiting for it to come down.

Nothing your opponents or your team may do can help you here. You must *immediately* move yourself ten metres from the opponent who is waiting for the ball, and fast.

If nobody is waiting for it, remove yourself from the spot where it's going to land. If events are moving so rapidly that you cannot *avoid* being less than ten metres from the opponent when he catches the ball (or from the spot where the ball lands), then just beat it as smartly as you can, and the referee won't say anything. However, as you depart, steer clear of your opponents, especially the man about to catch the ball. If you find yourself between him and his goal-line – that is, on the upfield side of the ten-metre circle – don't run across the centre of the circle in order to make your escape. Take the shortest route out. Look where your opponents are and avoid them, even if it means running to one side.

It's worth repeating. When you are offside under the Ten-Metre Law there is only one thing to do: immediately and quickly retire

The Ten-Metre Law: Act 1: Beat it! An offside player must not stay within 10 metres of an opponent waiting to catch the ball. Until he's moved outside that 10-metre circle, nothing his opponent does can put him onside.

ten metres from the waiting opponent. It's worth repeating because what you *must* do is not what you *want* to do. Here is an opponent waiting to catch the ball, and here you are near enough to close in and clobber him or at least to hang around and look threatening; naturally you don't want to run away. It's a strange and unnatural reaction. But it's what the law says you must do, and do at once. This is the only occasion in the game of rugby when the ball is in open play and you are required to run *away* from the action. The habit does not come easily. You just have to work at it.

Onside under the Ten-Metre Law

Retiring ten metres does not, of course, automatically put you onside and therefore back in the game. All it does is keep you out of trouble. If you don't retire ten metres you are *criminally* offside, and liable to be penalised. After you've retired ten metres you may still be offside, depending on what else has happened in the game, but at least you're safe.

While you *are* retiring ten metres, the only way you can become onside is through your own efforts or the efforts of an onside team-mate: either you can run behind him or he can run in front of you; it adds up to the same thing. So if he follows up fast enough, you might not need to cover the full ten metres.

Suppose, for instance, that you are in front of your full-back when he puts up a high kick ahead. You discover that you are only a few feet from an opponent who is getting ready to catch the ball, so you immediately turn and run. Meanwhile, your full-back has

White kicks and follows up

The Ten-Metre Law: Act 2: Onside is possible again. Once an offside player has obeyed the Ten-Metre Law, he can be put onside by a team-mate or an opponent, in any of the usual ways.

been hotly pursuing his kick, and before you've had time to cover more than about five metres, he passes you. This puts you onside; you can stop beating it and join in the game again.

Once you *have* retired the full ten metres, you're in the same position as any other offside player, so you can be put onside by your opponents as well as by your team-mate. If one of them runs five metres with the ball, or kicks or passes or drops it, or intentionally touches it, you can go straight back into the game. But *until* you've retired your ten metres, nothing your opponents do can put you onside. Nothing.

The reason why

The Ten-Metre Law makes sense. As an offside player you must not take any part in the game; and your opponent cannot be expected to concentrate on catching a greasy ball coming out of the sun if you're standing right next to him, breathing hard. Of course, *you* know you're offside, so *you* know that you are not going to lay a finger on him. But *he* doesn't know that, and your magnetic presence might make him nervous. Or you might accidentally get in his way. Or simply not get *out* of his way. So the laws say you *must* get out of his way *before* he gets the ball and keep on getting out of it until you're ten metres off.

There's one small exception to this. Suppose an attacking player kicks the ball, an opponent charges it down, and another attacking player who is within ten metres of the opponent plays the ball. No crime has been committed. The opponent wasn't *waiting to play the ball*, so the Ten-Metre Law doesn't apply; and the second attacker was put onside when the opponent intentionally touched the ball.

Two rules to remember

1 If you are offside and less than ten metres from an opponent waiting to catch the ball, you can never be put onside by any action of your opponents, so don't wait for it. Don't wait for anything. Clear off.

2 Any *other* time you are offside in open play, you are *always* put onside the moment an opponent kicks, passes or intentionally touches the ball. (But see Chapter 9.)

The penalty for offside

There are, in fact, *two* penalties for offside play, and the unpenalised side can choose which one it wants.

You will remember (how could you ever forget?) that you are penalised for offside when you are in front of a player on your own team who has the ball or last played it, and you try to take part in the game.

Now the penalty – and pay attention, because this isn't as easy as the rest – the penalty can be *either* a penalty kick where you (the offside player) took part in the game *or* a scrum where he (your team-mate) last played the ball.

Remember that it takes two to make offside – you, and your mate who had the ball behind you – and the penalty is either a kick where you are now, or a scrum where he was then.

If this all sounds a bit overdone, believe me that it makes good sense in practice, and it's worth understanding, because one day you might be captain of a team when an opponent gets done for being offside and the referee will look you straight in the eyes and say: 'Kick or scrum?' And if you shrug your shoulders and say you haven't the faintest idea, the ref is going to give you a very old-fashioned look and the selectors are going to give you a very modern rocket.

Here are two examples which show you how the kick-here-or-scrum-there penalty works out. Blues are playing Whites.

1 From a scrum on the Whites' 22-metre line, Blues win the ball, which goes to the Blue fly-half. He kicks ahead, not very well, and a White player catches the ball. A Blue forward who is in front of the kicker (and therefore offside) makes a tackle. Now Whites can *either* take a penalty kick where the Blue forward went wrong *or* a scrum at the place where the Blue fly-half kicked ahead. Since the scrum would give them only a few extra metres, and since they are defending, they probably choose the penalty kick.

2 Near his own goal-line, the Blues' full-back kicks for touch, misses, and the ball goes to a White player. A Blue player is less

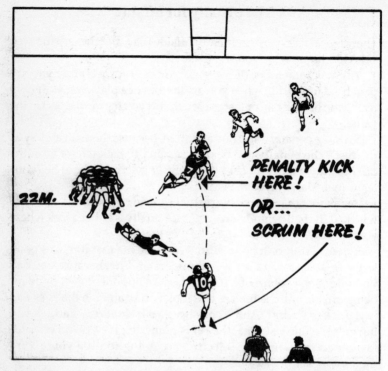

Penalty for offside play: kick or scrum? The Black flanker, obviously offside, tackles an opponent. The referee offers the White team a choice: either a scrum where the kick was made, or a penalty kick where the tackle happened. They probably take the kick.

than ten metres from him. He makes no effort to retire and he's penalised for offside under the Ten-Metre Law. Whites can take *either* a penalty kick where the offside Blue player was standing *or* a scrum where the Blue full-back kicked. The penalty kick would be in mid-field, perhaps too far out for Whites to kick a goal, but the scrum would be near their opponents' goal-line; so Whites might well choose the scrum.

Penalty for offside play: scrum or kick? A big kick by the Black full-back finds a team-mate, miles offside, about to clobber an opponent. Whites' choice is either a penalty kick where the player was offside (midfield) or a scrum where the ball was kicked, near the posts. They might prefer the scrum.

Accidental offside

What happens to a player who is offside, who is really sincerely making every effort not to interfere with the game, but who, despite himself, gets involved in it? (For instance, when a team-mate who has the ball bumps into him.)

You will be relieved to hear that the laws treat him with dignity and restraint. Provided the referee is satisfied that the team in possession gained no advantage from the accidental offside, he lets play go on. If, on the other hand, he considers that it has improved their chances, he orders a scrum, with their opponents putting the ball in.

Readers write

P.J. of Swansea writes: What if a player kicks ahead and then runs forward to put his team onside, but he does his running in touch? Is that OK?

D.R. There's nothing to stop him running in touch (or even in touch-in-goal), but in order to put a player onside the runner must be in the playing area.

P.J. Why?

D.R. Because that's where the game is played, dummy.

*   *   *

M.N.T. of Wimbledon writes: This is about the Ten-Metre Law. Suppose the player waiting to catch the ball is standing a yard from touch, and there's an opponent right next to him. If that opponent steps into touch, he can't be penalised for being within ten metres, can he?

D.R. Who says?

M.N.T. A bloke I met in the pub.

D.R. The whole point of the Ten-Metre Law is to make sure an opponent can't influence the catcher by being, or staying, near him. If this opponent steps into touch, I'd advise him to keep moving.

M.N.T. The ref might penalise him for leaving the field without permission.

D.R. Nobody said life was easy.

3
The tackle

One of the big things about rugby, as we never tire of repeating, is that it should be fast-moving and continuous, with as few stoppages as possible.

On the other hand, the big thing about the tackle is that it latches on to something that is moving fast and stops it dead.

Clearly, tackles must be made; but then the game must go on. That is what the law of the tackle tries to bring about. This, too, is quite simple, as long as you know *what is a tackle and what is not*.

For a start, a tackle must be in the field-of-play (the stretch between the goal-lines). You can't be tackled in an in-goal. Brought down, yes. Tackled, no.

Tackled: ball touches ground. If the ball-carrier is held by an opponent in the field-of-play, and the ball touches the ground, then he's been tackled.

Tackled: player on one knee. If the ball-carrier is held by an opponent in the field-of-play, and he's on one knee (or both knees), then he's been tackled.

If a player with the ball, in the field-of-play, is held by an opponent and brought down, he's tackled. It's very straightforward. Grab the ball-carrier and bring him to earth, and the law says you've tackled him.

What the law actually says in so many words is that he's tackled if he is held and 'brought to the ground or the ball comes into contact with the ground.' You might think the ball couldn't touch the ground unless the player holding it had also been brought down, but believe me, anything's possible.

If you want to know what 'brought to ground' means, it means 'no longer on his feet', which is probably what you thought it meant. But what if he's on one foot and one knee? Or on both knees? Or sitting on his duff? Or on top of another player who is on the ground? Has he been brought to ground and therefore tackled? Yes, he has. 'On his feet,' say the laws, means 'on both his feet'. If he's not up he's down. Simple as that.

Lifting the ball-carrier off his feet is not a tackle.

Immediately you're tackled, both you and the tackler must try to make the ball available so that play can go on.

The key words in the tackle law are *held* and *brought to ground*. One is no good without the other. If a player dives at an opponent and knocks him over without holding him, it's not a tackle, and so the opponent need not let go of the ball. He must do *something* – he can't just lie there, thinking beautiful thoughts – but he's free to throw the ball to a team-mate, or to get up and run with it. In this situation, there is nothing to stop him passing off the ground: nothing.

The working of the tackle law is really very simple and obvious. When play can reasonably go on, the law lets it go on. When the tackled player hits the deck, it makes him let go of the ball so that someone else can play it. Immediately.

There are two reasons why the laws says *immediately*. One is so that other players can grab the ball and keep the game going. The other is so that you aren't turned into a basket case by opponents who are looking for the ball. As usual, what's good for the game is good for the player, too.

Hang on. Not so fast. Let's go back a bit. The tackled player must make the ball available. What exactly does *available* mean?

It certainly means a lot more than just letting go of the ball.

If you're tackled, the laws allow you to *pass* the ball provided you do it immediately. (Hard to imagine a player passing the ball the instant he hit the deck because his legs had been scythed from under him; but there are other forms of tackle. A tackled player on

Tackled: lying on another player. If the ball-carrier is held by an opponent in the field-of-play and he's lying on another player (including that opponent), then he's been tackled.

one knee might be able to get an immediate pass away.)

Or the laws allow you to *release* the ball provided you do it immediately and then get up or get out of the way if you can. The word 'release' has an interesting pair of meanings. You can release the ball by *putting it on the ground in any direction*. Or you can release it by *pushing it along the ground in any direction*, except (of course) forward.

You may have noticed that the direction preferred by most tackled players is towards their own team.

Right then, onwards. You are tackled, you let go of the ball. Fine. What next?

The next player to play the ball – whether he picks it up, passes it or kicks it – *must be on his feet*. Rugby is a game where you run with the ball, and you can't run on your knees. That goes for you, for the man who tackled you, and for anyone else who turns up. Find your feet before you look for the ball.

Normally, of course, the tackler and the tackled man have their faces in the mud, so it's the third man up who gets the ball. This player has achieved mythic status in refereeing circles. 'Third man

Tackled: sitting. If the ball-carrier is held by an opponent in the field-of-play, and he's sitting on the ground, then he's been tackled.

Third man up must be on his feet. After a tackle, the next man to play the ball must be on his feet and stay on his feet.

up must be on his feet,' referees tell anyone who will listen. When the ball gets released from a tackle, the referee takes a keen interest in the next man to play the ball. Never mind how far the ball may be from the tackle – if the next man is not on his feet, or if he was on his feet until he dived on the ball, the referee hammers him. This makes sense. When the tackled player makes the ball available but the next man up promptly makes it unavailable, play grinds to a halt.

The tackle law is very simple. If you're not on your feet after a tackle, you can't do anything. You can't play the ball. You can't even touch it. You can't tackle an opponent who gets the ball. You can't even *try* to tackle him. There's only one thing you *can* do: get up. So do it.

Tacklers: now hear this!

What's sauce for the ball-carrier is sauce for the tackler. If they both go to ground with the ball, the tackler must act fast. He must let his opponent release the ball. In fact the tackler must completely let go of the tackled player, and do so at once. Then he must get away from him, and from the ball. If he can get up, he should get up, for the very good reason that he can't play the ball until he's on his feet. Both players – the tackler and the tackled man – have a duty to make the ball available, by releasing it and getting clear of it. (But note that if the tackled player is lying within reach of a goal line, an opponent can legally pull the ball from his hands to prevent a try or touch-down.)

Scoring while tackled

You can score a try even though you are tackled. If sheer momentum takes you from the field-of-play to the goal-line, dragging the tackler behind you, certainly you can score. Alternatively you can reach out and score even if the tackle has stopped you dead, just short of the line – provided you do it immediately. Full details are in the chapter on Scoring.

Brief reminder

None of the above applies to the in-goal. A tackle, legally speaking, is only a tackle in the field-of-play, which is the area between the goal-lines. Once you cross the goal-line there is not much point in expecting a bloke to drop the ball just because you've got hold of him, so the law is completely different there. (See the chapter on in-goal play.)

Tackling has not always been the humane and enlightened affair it is today. Back in the 1850s, when the game was still a kind of student demonstration at Rugby School, a player who was 'collared' could cry, 'Have it down!' and put the ball on the ground for a scrum. If he didn't, his opponents could shout 'Hack him over!' and start kicking. They hacked only from the knee down, and they weren't allowed to hold *and* hack at the same time; still, they sometimes hacked for up to a quarter of an hour before they got the ball down. Today's law achieves the same result about three hundred times more rapidly and five thousand times less painfully.

The penalty for breaking any part of the tackle law is a penalty kick where it happened.

Readers write

Q.W. of Bristol writes: That stuff you wrote about tackles and what should happen next, I mean it's all very nice and neat, but it's not what actually happens, is it?

D.R. Isn't it?

Q.W. Not in top matches, no. A bloke gets tackled and his mates arrive at high speed and they go straight past him and drive into any opponents and knock them down before they can get near the ball. It's like American football.

D.R. Well, it's illegal.

Q.W. So why isn't it penalised?

D.R. I was hoping you were going to tell me.

* * *

P.O'B. of Belfast writes: What's all that malarkey about a tackled player being allowed to pass the ball?

D.R. It's in the laws.

P.O'B. He's lying on the ground, and he can still pass the ball? Even though he's tackled? Come off it.

D.R. Yes, he can. Provided he does it immediately.

P.O'B. How quick is immediately?

D.R. Quick as you can. Suppose you're holding a hot potato. How quickly would you let it go? Well, that's immediately.

P.O'B. Is it an Irish potato?

* * *

A.H. of Edinburgh writes: You said a tackled player can release the ball by putting it on the ground.

D.R. That's right.

A.H. But he doesn't, does he?

D.R. Tell me more.

A.H. He puts the ball on the ground but he doesn't release it! He keeps his hand on top of it. He holds it steady for a team-mate to pick up.

D.R. It's a wicked world we live in.

4
The player and the ball on the ground

Forget tackles. This has nothing to do with being tackled or making a tackle. This is about what happens when a player with the ball goes to ground, or when a player goes to ground in order to gather the ball, and what he must do next.

He must act immediately.

Falling on the ball – for instance, to stop a forward rush – is all right. Lying on the ball stops the entire game, and is all wrong.

Once you've gone to ground and got the ball, it doesn't much

Don't lie on or around the ball. It's not enough to avoid lying on the ball – you must also do all you can to get up or roll away from it. This player isn't touching the ball, but he's obviously obstructing others who want to get at it.

matter what you do as long as you do it at once. You have a small choice. You can either get to your feet with the ball, or pass it or release it while you're on the ground. And if you pass or release it, you must also get up or move away from it, immediately.

The All Blacks, who are a poetic lot, have a charming couplet:

Do not lie upon the grass,
You cannot ruck when on your arse.

Don't tell me that it doesn't rhyme, or that they are daft about rucking in New Zealand. The verse tells an eternal truth, which is that rugby is meant to be played by players who are on their feet. Anyone who makes the ball unplayable by falling down, or by staying down, is bad news.

Don't lie near the ball

If you're not going to play the ball, you must, if you can, get up or roll away from it. What you must *not* do is drape yourself around the ball and lie there until help comes. Even if you are the last defender and the enemy is two feet from your line, you must not lie on the ball. It ruins the game and – unless the referee blows up smartly – it may do considerable damage to you, too.

Don't fall over a player with the ball

If you can't lie near the ball, then it's no surprise that intentionally falling over a player on the ground with the ball (or near the ball) is just as bad. The key words are 'intentionally falling'. That's what the referee is liable to penalise. The moral is: make an effort to stay on your feet. After all, that's where the game is played.

5
Somebody blundered: Part I

Four principles sum up the things you must and must not do in rugby:

1 The only way to gain ground is to run or kick. You must not throw or knock the ball forward.
2 You can grab an opponent, or get in his way, only if he has the ball.
3 Even so, you must not play dangerously.
4 You must do all you can to keep the game as fast-moving and continuous as possible.

If you follow these simple principles, you'll be all right – in theory. Still, it won't do any harm to go through the charge sheet with a powerful lens and a fine-tooth comb.

Throw-forward and knock-on

Penalty: scrum.

Throw-forward

You must not throw the ball forward. 'Forward' does not mean 'in front of you'; it means 'towards the enemy line'. (If you have crossed the enemy line and are unselfishly donating the ball to a team-mate, just don't throw it towards the enemy dead-ball line.) Picture an imaginary line running through the ball, parallel to the goal lines, and make your pass go along or behind that line, and you should be all right. If the ball hits the ground and *bounces* forward, your pass is still okay. The laws try to regulate what you do, but nobody on earth can say what a rugby ball is going to do next. If you make a pass which starts travelling through the air quite legally but then gets blown forward by the wind, it too is okay.

It has been argued by people who have nothing better to do, that when two players are running upfield absolutely level with each other and one gives a pass, the ball must go forward if it is to arrive where and when the other player is due to arrive, even though the first player is still running level with him. Other people disagree, and draw little diagrams with their beer on the top of the bar to prove it by trigonometry.

It doesn't matter terribly much, because when you start cutting it as fine as that, the decision really hinges on how much dust there is in the referee's left eye. That's where all the really important trigonometry takes place. It doesn't much matter whether or not you make a forward pass – what matters is whether the referee *thinks* you did. Moral: make it easy for him to approve.

One tiny detail: if you hand the ball to another player, this is a pass. If the player is in front of you, he's offside and the upshot is a scrum for accidental offside, unless he did it on purpose, in which case it's a penalty kick.

Knock-on

If you can't *throw* the ball forward, then you must not *knock* it forward, either. Stands to reason. To qualify for a knock-on, you don't actually have to *knock* the ball, or punch it, prod it or even give it a good hard slap. A knock-on need be nothing more than a clumsy fumble in the general direction of the enemy camp.

A knock-on needs three things. First, the ball hits your hand or arm (or vice versa). Second, it goes forward: towards the enemy's dead-ball line. (You can knock-on in his In-goal, remember.) Third, you fail to catch it again before it touches the ground or another player.

The knock-on law isn't interested in distance. A knock-on is a knock-on, whether the scrum-half nudged the ball half an inch or the winger elbowed it six feet. Furthermore, the law doesn't care how many times you lose the ball. Whether you're fielding a kick or taking a pass or scooping the ball up from the ground, you can fumble and juggle it till your captain's hair turns white, but provided you don't drop it altogether or let it touch another player, this is not a knock-on.

Exception: charged-down kick

If you succeed in charging down an opponent's kick, this is not a knock-on – even if the ball hits your hand or arm and goes forward and hits the ground – provided you didn't try to catch the ball. If you succeeded in catching the ball you must have bionic eyes and hands like flypaper.

No deliberate knock-ons

The laws say that a knock-on (or a throw-forward, come to that) must be unintentional. If you interrupt an enemy pass by sticking your great fist out and deliberately knocking the ball forward, you're asking for trouble. Similarly, if you see the opposition coming at you from all sides and you get rid of the ball by throwing it forward, that's bad news. In either case the penalty is a penalty kick and the referee may even award a penalty try.

Knock-on: second bite at the cherry. If you accidentally knock the ball forward, but you catch it before it touches the ground or another player, then this is not an infringement, and play goes on.

Charge-down: not a knock-on. If you charge down a kick and knock the ball forward, this is not an infringement, and play goes on (provided you didn't try to catch the ball).

Out there in the sweat and mud of battle, nobody talks about a throw-forward. Everyone calls it a forward pass – everyone but the lawbook, and the lawbook has a good reason. A pass involves two players. A throw-forward does not. The law doesn't care what you are trying to do, or whether you have a team-mate at the other end of it. If the ball leaves your hands and it's thrown forward, that's enough.

Mind you, I have seen players claim that a throw-forward was really a knock-on, and not even that, because they caught the ball, sir. (Players always say 'sir' to the ref when they're on dodgy ground.) What happened was the player reached far behind him to take a terrible pass, biffed the ball ten feet forward, and ran on and caught it. Nice try. But if the ref says that it was a throw-forward, you'd better believe him.

If you must fumble, fumble backwards

A knock-on does not have to be knocked, but it does have to be *on*. Suppose you take a pass or field a kick when you are facing backwards, towards your own line. You can juggle with the ball, fumble it, drop it and it's all perfectly legal. The game goes on. Unless the ball bounces *forward* – towards the enemy line – from a hand or arm, then it's not a knock-on.

A couple of laughably obvious points which nobody but a raving perfectionist like yourself would bother to read:

A rebound – off the chest, for example, or the shoulder – is not a knock-on; it's a rebound. If, however, a rebound ricochets off a chest and hits a hand or arm *and then* bounces forward, it *is* a knock-on. What often happens is that a player fails to catch a ball, which hits his chest and bounces forward, leaving him wheezing pitifully, the spectators demanding a knock-on, and the referee, quite rightly, doing nothing. Incidentally, it's perfectly legal to *head* the ball in rugby. You can even head the ball forward, into touch. I saw it done once, in an international match. By Gareth Edwards of Wales. Very enterprising fellow, Gareth.

In case you have just joined us at this point, here is a news summary. A player throws-forward or knocks-on when he throws or knocks (or even fumbles) the ball in the direction of his opponents' dead-ball line – unless (in the case of a knock-on) he catches it again before it touches the ground or another player. The penalty for this lapse is a scrum where it happened, with his opponents getting the put-in.

And now, back to our regular programme.

Readers write

L.C. of Leicester writes: Last week I saw the referee explaining the tackle law to the captains. I was brought up to believe he wasn't allowed to do any coaching before the match. Has that been changed?

D.R. No. 'Coaching' means giving tactical advice before the match, and referees are not allowed to do that; but they are allowed to give *instructions* to the teams in advance, especially if this will increase the players' safety. The tackle law is a good example.

6

Somebody blundered: Part II

Foul play

The Foul Play Law has three separate parts: (1) Obstruction, (2) Unfair Play and Repeated Infringements, and (3) Dangerous Play and Misconduct.

Now that's a mouthful. Some bits stick in the throat more than others. The difference between them tells us a lot about the laws and what they're out to do.

Take **Obstruction** (example: running in front of a team-mate carrying the ball). This is trying to play the right game in the wrong way. If caught, you get penalised with a penalty kick.

Next is **Unfair Play** (example: throwing the ball into touch) and **Repeated Infringements** (example: persistently feeding the scrum crookedly). This is all about distorting or evading the laws, not necessarily with physical violence. If caught, you get penalised with a penalty kick. Keep it up and you might get sent off.

Last and worst is **Dangerous Play** (example: late tackle) and **Misconduct** (example: taunting an opponent after you've scored.) This is not playing the game at all. If you're lucky you only get warned and penalised with a penalty kick. Do it again and , if you're lucky, you get penalised with a penalty kick (perhaps even a penalty try), exiled to the changing room, and eventually carpeted before the Disciplinary Committee. (If you're unlucky you get a large knuckle sandwich from the opposition. The laws forbid retaliation, but don't push your luck.)

This three-way split reflects the aims of the Foul Play Law.

The laws as a whole are against wrongdoing, and wherever it rears its ugly head the lawbook delivers a crisp penalty kick or free kick. But if the player was taking an active part in the game when he committed Obstruction, the laws consider a penalty kick enough. 'The lad did wrong,' they reason patiently, 'but at least he wanted to get on with the game. Now perhaps he'll know better.'

By contrast, anyone guilty of Unfair Play or Repeated Infringements is trying to rewrite the lawbook in his own favour – for instance, by persistently getting offside at scrums or line-outs. The laws take a dim view, and they discourage him with a penalty kick. 'Change your ways,' they add, 'or we might be obliged to dispense with your services altogether.'

The really big guns come out against Dangerous Play (such as kicking an opponent) or Misconduct (such as kicking him while the ball is out of play). This isn't mild cheating by someone who doesn't understand the game. This is a bloke being so stupid, negative and pernicious that he's really sabotaging the game. He's not so much playing bad rugby as playing anti-rugby, so he's a menace to all concerned. The laws not only penalise him with a penalty kick but also require the referee to warn him. If he commits a similar offence (note that word *similar*: it doesn't have to be precisely the same offence), then the laws say he *must* be sent off. If his first offence was bad enough, he can be sent off there and then, without warning.

Rugby is a tough, physical game. It demands self-discipline. The laws come down hard on a player who can't control himself. 'That joker is going to spoil it for everyone,' they brood, worriedly. 'If he wants to indulge his sordid whims he'd better take up alligator-wrestling. Next time he tries to throttle the scrum-half, have him quietly removed.'

Obstruction

1 Running for the ball

When you are running for the ball, and an opponent is also running for the ball, you must not charge him or push him *except shoulder to shoulder*. Now, you very rarely see this shoulder-to-shoulder stuff done, and when you do somebody in the crowd usually takes exception to it; nevertheless it's perfectly legal as long as you keep running for the ball. It can be very effective, too, especially if the other bloke trips over his own feet.

Shoulder-to-shoulder charging is legal. If you and an opponent are both running for the ball, it's perfectly legal to charge him – but it must be shoulder-to-shoulder and you must keep running while you do it.

2 Offside player obstructing opponent

If you are in front of a player on your own side who has the ball (which makes you offside, right?), you must not stand or move in such a way that you obstruct an opponent who's trying to get at him. This is pretty obvious: if you're offside, you have no business interfering with the course of the game, and here you are, blocking the tackle.

Notice that it's up to you to *avoid* interfering with play. It is possible to obstruct an opponent simply by *being* in his way as well as by *getting* in his way. If you're offside and in his way at all, it's your job to get out of it – not his job to go around you.

3 Obstruction during a kick-ahead

The high kick-ahead is a tactic you often see in rugby. Usually a defender is waiting to catch the ball, while opponents are racing towards him. So far, so good. Trouble arises when team-mates

Blocking the tackle, a.k.a. 'scissoring'. If a player moves or stands in front of a team-mate who has the ball, so as to prevent an opponent from getting to him, that's obstruction – called 'scissoring' because the obstructing player often crosses the path of the ball-carrier.

appear in front of the catcher. They zigzag busily, running back and forth as if pursued by bees. What they are doing is making it difficult for opponents to reach the ball or the catcher. This is obstruction, and illegal. So is standing in front of (and near to) the catcher. This amounts to forming a shield to protect him.

4 Running into your own scrum or line-out

If you have the ball after a scrum or line-out, you must not try and crash through your own forwards in front of you. Same applies to ruck or maul. It's obvious: they must be offside, and you are bringing them into the game. Slightly less obviously, you are using them as a shield to keep the horny hands of the enemy off you; and since in rugby every man should be free to grab the man with the ball, provided he can catch him, what you are doing is wrong. Nevertheless, it's amazing how many players cannot resist taking the shortest route to the enemy line by ploughing straight through their own forwards.

Incidentally, the laws have laid down that a player carrying the ball can never be penalised for obstruction. If anyone gets penalised it's the team-mate he runs into.

5 Flanker swinging out from a scrum

When your side has hooked the ball in a scrum and it is coming out of the back row, the flanker – the man the laws call 'outside player' – must not swing further outwards to stop the opposing scrum-half

Flanker obstructs scrum-half. A flanker (No. 6 here) must not swing out from the scrum in order to prevent the opposing scrum-half from getting past him. The flanker can pack at any angle, but he must not then widen the angle.

from coming round and zeroing in on your scrum-half (if he's got the ball) or the ball itself (if he hasn't).

There's nothing, except the length of his arms, to stop a flanker from packing on to the scrum at a wide angle if he wants to. The law simply says that, once the ball has been heeled, he must not move out to an even wider angle.

And there's another side to that coin. The flanker must not swing out to obstruct the scrum-half, but equally that scrum-half must not lay hands on the flanker – or any opposing forward – to give himself leverage as he follows the ball when it's being heeled through the scrum. Handling a flanker like this is misconduct, for which the punishment is a penalty kick.

Unfair play

Unfair play is what happens when a player plays unfairly. And if you think that's a pretty broad definition, well, so it is. The Unfair Play Law is one of those handy catch-all regulations that the referee can call upon in an emergency. Such as…

1 Offending on purpose

A player who intentionally breaks any law is guilty of Unfair Play. Referees, you see, have the power to look into men's souls and divine their intentions.

Sometimes that intention is pretty obvious. Suppose you get the ball inside your 22 at a moment when five hulking opponents are bearing down on you. You've just sprained your ankle, so it seems unlikely that you will jink past them all. Inevitably, you will get flattened, they will get the ball, and after that, nothing stands between them and your goal line but twenty feet of autumn mist.

Suddenly you see a team-mate to your right. He's ten feet in front of you, but unmarked. If you give him a forward pass the referee is bound to notice, and a scrum will at least give your team a chance to re-group. So you cleverly throw the ball forward.

The referee whistles and gives your opponents a penalty kick, maybe even a penalty try. Rugby works on the assumption that players try to uphold the laws, even when they're feeling desperate.

Intentionally breaking a small law is a big deal. The Foul Play Law says a player must not intentionally infringe any Law of the Game. Here you see a player, about to be overwhelmed by opponents, intentionally throwing the ball forward in the hope of getting a scrum. A penalty kick is more likely; perhaps even a penalty try.

If you intentionally break a law for which the usual penalty is only a scrum, you are distorting the game, and you'll be made to pay for it.

2 Time-wasting

Wasting time is a fairly pointless way to behave; if you don't want to play, what are you doing out there in the first place? Especially as the referee is going to penalise you for unfair play. Let's face it, intentional time-wasting is hard to hide. Throwing the ball in the wrong direction when your opponents have been given a penalty kick is an obvious delay. So is not forming a scrum or a line-out. So is delaying a drop-out. The penalty is at least a free kick. It might be a second penalty kick, and a penalty try is not impossible.

That's *intentional* time-wasting. There is also the other kind, of which quite a lot goes on. Some players waste time simply by not doing all they could to get on with the game. There is a slow way to put the ball into a scrum, and a fast way. The slow way is for the forwards to pack down and the scrum-half to start looking for the ball. When he locates it – cleverly camouflaged on that patch of mud, ten yards away – he *walks* over to it, picks it up, drops it, retrieves it, reads the name on it in case it's the wrong ball, and *walks* slowly back to the scrum.

Correct me if my arithmetic is wrong; but that leaves sixteen forwards heaving and sweating, and thirteen backs standing around scratching themselves, while one scrum-half carries on the game at a steady limp. I don't care if he is getting his breath back, it's still a pathetic waste of twenty-nine players' time. What's more, it is, strictly speaking, illegal.

The laws are liberally spattered with the key phrase, 'without delay'. The ball must be put into the scrum without delay. In fact, the laws say that it shall be put in without delay *as soon as the two front rows have closed together*. So any scrum-half who waits until a flanker has finished blowing his nose and leaned on the nearest rump before he puts the ball in, is wasting time. Any hooker who has a lengthy discussion (or even two) about the line-out signal, before throwing in the ball, is wasting time. Any team which is awarded a penalty kick and then democratically debates what to do with it, is wasting time. Nobody ever scored a try while the ball was out of play.

I am not suggesting that everything should be done at a gallop. All I'm saying is that, if players were as alert when the ball is dead as they are when it's alive, then we would see shorter stoppages and more game. (Amazingly, even at international level, the ball is actually in play for only about one-third of the game.) As it is, they often regard the sound of the whistle as a signal to stop thinking.

The referee has a duty, under the laws, to see that the game goes forward 'without delay', and if he thinks you're acting unnecessarily sluggishly, he is right to award a free kick just to goose you along a bit. And the fact that you didn't *know* you were acting all constipated is neither here nor there: one disadvantage of sluggishness is that very often you're too sluggish to realize just how sluggish you are.

3 Throwing into touch

Intentionally throwing (or knocking) the ball into touch is also Unfair Play. If you want to put the ball into touch you must either kick it there or take it there in person. Throwing into touch is the easy way out. This also applies to intentionally throwing the ball into touch-in-goal or over the dead-ball line. The penalty is a penalty kick.

If, however, you try to give a pass to a team-mate who turns out to be not there, and you throw the ball straight into touch, this is not intentional, so you won't be penalised.

Persistent offending

Or, as the laws call it, Repeated Infringement. This is pretty basic stuff. The laws of rugby are a description of the game. Change the description and you change the game.

Players who persistently break a law are, in effect, trying to change the game. They may be doing it for their own advantage, for example, by barging in the line-out. Or they may be doing it simply because they don't know any better. (There are hookers like that.) The effect is the same: it distorts the game, and by distorting it, ruins it for everyone. The prop forward who won't let the ball into the scrum is damaging the chances of *both* teams to get on with the game. Ignorance is no excuse: the damage is the same whether he knows what he's doing, or not.

That is why the referee is given large powers to deal with this sort of thing. Not surprisingly, he is required to apply a stricter standard in senior matches: when a player breaks the same law for the third time, the referee must warn him about it, and if that doesn't work he can even send him off. In more junior rugby, where the percentage of dipsticks is higher, the referee usually warns the player first and then, if he doesn't improve, warns his captain that the player will have to go off unless he can be rendered harmless. The captain, if he has any brains, gives the offender an immediate posting to the wing, followed by an early lesson on the game.

Certain problem areas seem to breed repeated infringements – the scrum, line-out, ruck/maul, and the offside laws. A set of backs who persistently wander over on to the wrong side of their offside line can stifle attack after attack. I know they get penalised, and that might mean three points against them, but then again it might not; and in any case their opponents would sooner have seven points from a converted try, thank you very much.

One difficulty is that sometimes it isn't always the same player getting offside. When the same offence is shared out by a team, what can the referee do? A great deal. He can take a long, cool look at the way a number of different players have committed the same offence, and if he decides that it adds up to repeated infringement, then he can give the team a general warning. After that he has no choice. The next player to repeat that offence – even if he personally is doing it for the first time – must be sent off. Referees are not out there to make friends. They're out there to apply the laws of the game, and the laws give them considerable muscle to do it.

Dangerous play

1 Don't strike an opponent

And it's no good saying you hit him because he wouldn't let go of the ball. You're not allowed to thump *any* opponent, with or without the ball, at *any* time.

Players on your own side are different, but not much. (I once reffed a match in which a captain whacked one of his forwards before I could penalise the chap for a minor piece of foul play; so I didn't.) There's no specific ban on clouting a team-mate, but the Foul Play law says you must not do anything against the spirit of good sportsmanship. Is it unsportsmanlike to give a colleague a poke in the chops? I suppose it might be. If he's smaller than you, for instance. On the whole, it's safer not to belt anyone.

2 Don't hack, kick, stamp on or trip anyone

That's pretty simple. It was not always so.

As late as 1866, all that the laws of the game as played at Rugby School said about hacking was that you could not do it on or above the knee or with the heel, and you couldn't hold *and* hack, unless, of course the victim stupidly refused to release the ball, in which case you could settle down and batter him to a pulp.

In 1874 the Rugby Football Union declared that hacking and tripping were absolutely prohibited under all circumstances, a sure sign that a lot of it was still going on.

Today, of course, hacking is definitely out … Well, let's not get carried away; you don't see many manufacturers of shin-pads selling matches in the street; so let's say that any hacking is accidental rather than intentional.

Then there's stamping.

While you contemplate the grisly spectacle of one player stamping on another, you might like also to ponder what the law of the land says about negligence.

It says that everybody has a duty of care to his neighbour. This means that you must not behave in such a way that another person gets hurt. Do something which you know might be harmful, and you're guilty of negligence. What's more, you're just as guilty if you don't know and you don't care whether or not it's harmful. So where does stamping fit in?

Take a player who treads on an opponent to make him release the ball. That player knows he's doing harm; he must know; he can

Reckless = dangerous = foul play. Dangerous use of the boot is banned. This includes – for example – taking a wild and reckless kick at the ball when it's close to an opponent. Dangerous play is not necessarily malicious. It can also be careless. Players have an obligation to avoid both.

see what he's doing. Now take another player who charges into a ruck and then tramples on an opponent who happens to be underfoot. This player can't see where his boots are going and he doesn't care, as long as he gives the ruck a good shove. Which player is guilty of stamping?

Both are.

The first player may claim he was simply trying to winkle out the ball, which his opponent should have moved away from, according to law. The second player may defend his action by saying he was half-buried in a ruck, so he couldn't be expected to know what his feet were doing, and anyway his opponent was offside.

Neither excuse holds water. An opponent's offence cannot justify dangerous play; and it's a player's responsibility to *know* where his boots are, and to control what they do. Any player who stamps on someone is acting recklessly. Boots, and especially studs, can do great damage.

This is one area where the laws of the game overlap with the laws of the land. You might have a rush of blood to the head and end up in court; maybe in jail. Others have. Remember that, when you put your boots on. It's a game. It's not a war.

Lastly, there's tripping. Tripping is done with the foot. If you trip over somebody's hand or arm, that's your fault, not his.

3 Do not tackle dangerously

What is or is not a dangerous tackle is a matter for the referee to decide, but I can tell you that there are five kinds which bring the whistle to his lips like a flash. They are: early tackling; late tackling; high tackling; tackling an opponent as he jumps for the ball; and stiff-arm tackling.

Early and late tackles are doubly illegal – you're playing the man without the ball – and they are dangerous because your opponent has no chance to brace his body for the impact. In this respect, a late tackle can be worse than an early one, because the player has *relaxed* after giving his pass.

A high tackle is a tackle above the ball-carrier's shoulders, known in the trade as 'clotheslining', because it has the same throttling effect as running into a clothesline. You must not tackle an opponent around his neck or head. That includes yanking him

Dangerous play. An early tackle – like this, before the opponent has caught the ball – is dangerous and illegal. So is a late tackle, after he's passed or kicked.

by the collar. It also includes *trying* to tackle high. Even if he dodges and you grab sweet fresh air, you can still get penalised for making the attempt.

If an opponent is jumping for the ball – at a line-out, say, or when fielding a kick – it is dangerous play to tackle him while his feet are off the ground. That includes tapping or pulling his feet or legs. Why? Because he might land on his head. Satisfied?

'Stiff-arm tackle' is a slightly misleading term. The tackler can do it to the ball-carrier – but the ball-carrier can do it to the tackler too, so sometimes it's not even a tackle. What happens is one player hits the other with a stiff arm. When the tackler does it, he usually sticks his arm out where the ball-carrier's head runs into it. When the ball-carrier does it, he usually whacks the tackler with a rigid forearm. Either way it's dangerous play.

Avoiding causing injury is one of the responsibilities of playing rugby. Nobody expects a tackle to be pleasant or even painless, and one of the hazards of jinking your way through for a brilliant solo try is getting rudely dumped on your ass in the middle of it. But let us remember why we are playing this game; what the object is. The

Dangerous play. A high tackle – around the neck or head – is dangerous and illegal. You must not grab an opponent above the line of his shoulders, or by his collar.

aim in rugby is to win the ball and score with it. You get no thanks and no points for putting a player out of action. It's getting the ball that counts.

Once you find yourself making a tackle *in order to injure the player*, instead of *in order to get the ball from him*, then you are heading for a disaster the memory of which may haunt you for the rest of your life.

4 Don't bulldoze

Tackling was invented to stop the man with the ball. If you don't try to grab him but you simply charge into him or knock him down, this is dangerous play. After all, you can damage a player just by bulldozing into him, especially when you're twice his size and four times his weight.

Dangerous play. Tackling a player while his feet are off the ground (because he's jumping to catch the ball) is dangerous and illegal. You must wait until he lands before you tackle him.

It's also possible for the ball-carrier to be guilty of dangerous play. Take the hand-off, which is normally used to fend off a would-be tackler from the side, not the front. If the ball-carrier finds an opponent dead ahead, and he runs at him with an arm stuck out like a battering ram, the referee might well judge that battering has no part in the game, and penalise him.

5. Don't obstruct him after he's kicked the ball

If you think you've been here before, well, you have. This is more of the same old stuff about not charging, tackling, holding, prodding, barging or in any way molesting a player who hasn't got the ball – in this case, an opponent who hasn't got it because he has just kicked it.

What is so special about this offence is the penalty: *either* a penalty kick at the place where you did it *or* a penalty kick at the spot where the ball comes down. Why should this be?

The thinking behind this law is as follows. Suppose you are a three-quarter belting down the wing, ball neatly tucked under the outside arm. Out of the corner of your eye you see an opponent, hurtling in for a tackle. Meanwhile, hobbling at top speed down the middle, as you know from past experience, is your entire pack of forwards, baying for blood. It is but the work of a moment to extract the ball from the armpit and cross-kick it smartly into their immediate future – say, about fifteen metres in front of them.

Eager to the point of rashness, of course, they are all slightly offside at the moment you kick the ball. Being decent, law-abiding types, they skid to a halt. So it's up to you to carry on flashing down the wing until you've caught up with them and put them onside.

Right now is when your opponent, foiled of his tackle, runs directly in your path. Obstruction, of course; but look at the effect! Not only has he stopped you from taking part in the game; he has

Obstructing the kicker: a choice of penalties. When a player kicks the ball, and is then obstructed by an opponent, that player's team can choose to take the penalty kick either where the obstruction happened or where the ball landed. Not much doubt which one they choose here.

also effectively stopped you from putting your forwards onside. So he has quietly killed your brilliant cross-kick, and with it perhaps a chance of a try. By God, skinning with a blunt putty-knife is too good for the swine.

What the law lays down, to discourage this kind of obstruction, is that the innocent party can choose to take its penalty kick in one of two places, as already described. If the player who obstructed the kicker did so to nullify a cross-kick, then the law makes sure he fails by giving his opponents the chance of a penalty kick in the middle, where the ball landed. On the other hand, it may be that the cross-kick was a wild one and came down in a poor place from which to take a penalty, so they have the option of taking it from the spot where the player was obstructed.

You can see this would work out just as well if the kicker put in a kick-ahead instead of a cross-kick, before he was obstructed. Also there's always the penalty-try law, which applies when foul play robs the attacking team of a probable try.

In case anybody is wondering what happens if the cross-kick or kick-ahead comes down close to touch, or in touch, the answer is the optional penalty kick is given 15 metres in from touch, opposite where the ball landed or crossed the touch line. And if the kick-ahead landed in the in-goal or touch-in-goal or on or over the dead-ball line, the optional penalty kick is given 5 metres from the goal line, opposite where the ball crossed that line, and at least 15 metres in from touch. Don't try to memorise this formula; you'll only strain your brains. Leave it to the referee. He knows his stuff.

One last thought about alleged obstruction after a player has kicked the ball, and also about alleged late tackles.

Sometimes the kicker invites trouble. He knows the tackler is closing in, and he delays his kick to the last micro-second. By then the tackler is flying. He's in mid-air. Don't ask him to go into reverse. Or perhaps he's square in the ball-carrier's path, poised and ready to try and charge down the kick if he can't make a head-on tackle. Next thing you know, the kicker's kicked and the tackler's tackled him. Or the kicker's kicked and he has instantly collided with his waiting opponent.

I don't think that was a late tackle; I think it was a late kick. I don't think the collision was obstruction; I think the kicker got his timing wrong. Tacklers have rights in this world, too, and kickers should not expect tacklers to do them the favour of backing off and giving them extra space and time to kick.

6. Don't touch him unless he's got the ball

This gets right to the heart of the matter. If rugby is to be a wide-open, man-to-man contest for a bit of streamlined leather, people have got to be free to try to intercept the ball (or the ball-carrier) just as fast as their puny limbs and wheezing lungs can carry them. What you cannot have is other players reaching and pawing at them, lurching into them and seizing handfuls of hair, clothing or fatty tissue, or simply sneaking up behind and unloading a large shove in the small of the back. I mean, it's hard enough to run right across a rugby field after a heavy meal and wearing someone else's

Off-the-ball obstruction. Except at scrums, rucks or mauls, it is illegal to hold, shove or interfere with any player who hasn't got the ball. That includes grabbing his jersey, his shorts, or even his hair. By law, it's dangerous play. Referees take it seriously.

boots, without being got at by some grasping saboteur who isn't even looking for the ball.

Similarly it is wrong to obstruct an opponent who hasn't got the ball and wants it, simply by being or getting in his way. Sometimes, of course, it's difficult to get *out* of his way until you know which way he's going; but not always. If you are standing right between him and your team-mate who has just caught the ball and fallen flat on his face with it, don't put your hands on your hips and wait to be asked to move. Just move.

Keen students of the printed word will be asking themselves, at this point, if they haven't been here before. Doesn't it all seem terribly familiar? A sense of what the French call *déjà vu*? (They play rugby too.) Well, yes and no. Our recent skirmish with the law of Obstruction included a warning against offside players obstructing opponents by getting or being between them and the ball. That's what you're thinking of. Why then, you ask, go over it all again? Two reasons.

First, there is a difference. The Obstruction offence talks about *offside* players who *obstruct* an opponent. The Dangerous Play offence covers *any* player, offside or on, who obstructs or *lays hands on* an opponent. Now this is much worse. It is at least understandable that an offside player – by definition usually in front of a team-mate with the ball – might get in an opponent's way. It's wrong and it can't be allowed to pass, but it's understandable. But a player who hasn't even the excuse of being offside, and who not only obstructs an opponent but actually tries to distract him from the game by using force – now there is a bloke who is asking for trouble. He's in line for a penalty kick plus a warning or even a sending-off. There is no room in the game for private revenge. If you can't get the man with the ball, then don't get anybody.

That's the second reason for re-hashing this subject. It is important because it is absolutely basic, and therefore worth repeating a few times. The simple charm of rugby is that anyone can lay claim to the ball, and everyone else enjoys the same freedom to go after him and get it back. Don't try and stop them.

And don't imagine you can get around the law by grabbing a player's jersey instead of the player. Clothing counts, too.

In fact it hurts to have to tell you that there is one occasion when you can, lawfully, hold an opponent who hasn't got the ball, and that is in a scrum, ruck or maul. In general play, you can also drag away a player lying near the ball – but not at a ruck or maul.

Don't get too excited about it, though. As privileges go, this is worth about as much as sitting next to the driver on the bus. Besides, your opponents can do it to you, too.

7 Don't collapse the scrum (or ruck, or maul)

Telling a forward not to collapse the scrum is like telling a human pyramid not to scratch itself: horribly obvious. And yet it needs to be said, because you do see forwards doing it, for instance when their opponents have won the ball and are trudging relentlessly towards a pushover try.

Well, it's no good; you must not intentionally collapse a scrum. (If you merely come to pieces under the strain, that's different.) It's dangerous, and it negates the whole purpose of having a scrum, which is to have a scrum until the scrum is over. In this respect it's rather like travelling on the Tube, going to cocktail parties, or making love: they're all scrums, and you simply have to see them through to the end.

8 Don't do anything dangerous

A few more insanities to avoid. Don't jump on a ruck or maul. Don't, if you are a front row of a scrum, rush against your opponents. Don't, if you are a front-row player, lift an opponent off his feet or force him up and out of the scrum, commonly called 'popping'. Once he's off his feet, he's helpless, and 'popping' him could seriously injure him. All these madnesses are classified as dangerous play and will get you penalised.

9 Don't retaliate

You must not do anything that is dangerous to an opponent. Sometimes it is difficult, I know; but the fact that some bloody idiot is behaving like a bloody idiot does not entitle you to behave like a bloody idiot. What's more, if the referee has penalised your opponent's idiocy, and you then retaliate, he may reverse his decision and penalise you instead. So keep your cool and collect the points. Winning is the best revenge.

10 'Flying Wedge' and 'Cavalry Charge' banned

Usually these tactics are used when the attacking team is awarded a kick near the goal line. For a 'Flying Wedge', they take a tap-kick, players bind onto the ball-carrier in a wedge formation, and they try to drive him over the line. For a 'Cavalry Charge', attacking players form a line across the field, some distance behind the kicker. At a signal, they charge forward, the ball is tap-kicked and one player takes a pass at speed. Both the 'Flying Wedge' and the 'Cavalry Charge' are dangerous and illegal at all age levels.

Misconduct

1. Do nothing contrary to good sportsmanship

As if you would.

2. Don't start anything while the ball is out of play

This is another of those splendidly vague laws which every civilized nation keeps tucked away in its hip pocket to deal with lunatics and hotheads. It simply says that, while the ball is out of play, you must not obstruct, or molest, or interfere with, or spit at, or denounce, or make up obscene limericks about, any opponent. Nor must you commit any sort of misconduct. (Try and get round *that*.)

The penalty kick is given not where the offence took place but where the ball would next have been brought into play. If, for instance, your opponents kicked the ball over your goal line and you touched it down, and an opponent came up and molested you right in the solar plexus, you would take the penalty kick from your 22-metre line, since you would otherwise have had a drop-out. If the ball goes into touch and there's some hanky-panky before it's thrown in, the penalty kick is given fifteen metres in from touch.

Finally – and just to lumber your echoing skull with some data which you will probably never use – if the referee gives a penalty kick, or awards a free kick, and an opponent blows a fuse before the kick is taken, the referee awards a second penalty kick, ten metres in front of the first kick, and this second kick replaces the first one.

In this and all other cases of Dangerous Play and Misconduct, the penalty kick is only half the penalty. The referee can send the player off, there and then. If not, he *must* warn him; and if the player does it again, he *must* send him off. That means he stays off for the rest of the game and, depending on the Disciplinary Committee's feelings, probably for several other games, too.

Footnote

Please note that, when it comes to deciding whether or not somebody blundered, there is only one judge of fact and of law during a match – the referee. The lawbook says so. Therefore you're wasting your time if you try to argue with him, because (a) he won't argue back and (b) he won't alter his decision. The laws say he *cannot* alter his decision, except in two cases, both involving a touch judge.

If the referee blows his whistle for something and then sees that a touch judge has his flag up, he can accept that the ball went into touch first and change his decision to a line-out. (Mind you, he can also overrule the touch judge.) In certain top fixtures, where the appointed touch judges are also qualified referees, they can help the referee by signalling if they see dangerous play or misconduct take place. When he next stops the game, he will go over and ask what happened, and then make his decision accordingly: but it's still his decision. Others may advise, but during a match the referee is the only judge of fact and law.

Readers write

A.W. of Llanelli writes: I know you're not supposed to charge an opponent who's got the ball. You're always supposed to tackle him. But it never gets penalised, does it?

D.R. That depends on the circumstances.

A.W. Well, years ago, in an international, J.P.R. Williams shoulder-charged the winger into touch. He had to. It was a try, otherwise.

D.R. You're saying he had no choice. Maybe – but bulldozing the ball-carrier when you could tackle him is still Foul Play.

---

* * *

J.W. of Hawick writes: Is it a high tackle when the ball-carrier ducks at the last second?

D.R. Let the ref decide.

J.W. I mean to say, the tackler might be six-foot-four while his opponent's only four-foot-six.

D.R. Then the tackler should bend his knees more, shouldn't he?

* * *

T.F. of Camborne writes: You're a bit hard on the scrum-half, ordering him to put in the ball as soon as he can. The scrum is the only chance the pack have to get their breath back. Give us a break, for Pete's sake.

D.R. Ho-hum.

* * *

M.F. of Dublin writes: For the love of Mike, why would anyone in his in-goal want to throw the blessed ball into touch-in-goal? Couldn't he just as easily touch it down?

D.R. Not if he was being held upright, like a statue.

M.F. Has that ever happened?

D.R. Everything has happened.

* * *

P.J. of Pontypool writes: I was amazed to read that the ref *must* warn a player whenever he sees dangerous play. A monumental punch-up is dangerous play, isn't it?

D.R. Sounds like it.

P.J. How often do you see the ref warn every player involved in a punch-up? Never.

D.R. Well, he can if he wants to, so don't be surprised if he does.

7
Scrums

Including offside

I could write a whole book on scrums, and most of it would be junk.

It's one part of the game that has been turned into a special subject all on its own. Some people become experts in the scrum the way others spend their lives learning all there is to know about wallpaper, or the sex-life of the bloater. And it's about as big a waste of time as eating gravy with your fork.

Scrums are very simple. There is no secret about them. You can understand all, provided you use a little common sense and remember the ancient Chinese saying:

Only reason for scrum is re-starting game quickly and fairly.

Now, then. If that is its purpose, what is its shape? We all know what a scrum looks like – eight compressed men growing shorter and wider in an effort to telescope eight other compressed men – but what must you have, and what can you do without? It is (as you're probably starting to discover) all quite simple.

What is a scrum?

A scrum must have eight players from each team: no more and no less. Each front row must have three players. Each second row must have two locks. Each lock shoves on and binds on the prop in front of him. The No.8 must bind on one or both of the locks. All eight players must stay bound until the scrum ends.

The scrum begins as soon as the two front rows come together. The law says that from this moment the scrum-half *shall* put the ball in *without delay*. If he hangs around, picking bits of mud off the ball and waiting for his hooker to get comfortable, he is wasting time. He should be penalised, with a free kick.

Players often get upset about this, and usually for one of two reasons. They argue either that the scrum-half has to trundle off and get the ball, which takes time, or that the back-row forwards have to get themselves sorted out, which also takes time.

Both observations are true as far as they go. What they overlook is the fact that scrum-halves and back-row forwards can hustle pretty damn fast when they really want to. If they would only put a bit of ginger into their trundling, then half a second after the Front

Bird's-eye view of a scrum. The scrum-half stands one metre from the tunnel, and puts in the ball along the middle line, which is directly underneath where the shoulders of the front rows meet. Props (1 and 3) bind on the hooker (2), who binds on them. Locks (4 and 5) bind on each other and shove on their front row. Flankers (6 and 7) bind on the locks and shove on the props. All players in the scrum must bind onto it, using the full length of the arm. It's not enough for a flanker to rest his hand on a player's back or grab a handful of jersey near the shoulder blades.

Five went down the other forwards would be bound onto them. And half a second later the scrum-half would have the ball in.

It all depends on your attitude. If you regard a scrum as a kind of tea-break – a chance to lean on someone and get your breath back – then obviously there is no hurry. If you regard it as a piece of well-greased machinery for getting the ball into play, then you want to see it working quickly. Without cursing in my uncontrollable fashion, the laws leave no doubt that they are against tea-breaks.

Who puts the ball in?

Let's leave abortive rucks and mauls aside for a minute. Apart from them, the team not responsible for the stoppage that led to the scrum is the team that puts the ball in. For instance, if a player knocks-on, his opponents get the put-in.

Where there's any doubt about which side caused the stoppage, the team that was moving forward before everything ground to a halt gets the put-in. If neither team was moving forward, the put-in goes to the attacking side.

If the referee stops play purely and simply for an injury, play restarts with a scrum. The team last in possession gets the put-in.

Scrum after ruck

If the ball gets stuck in a ruck, the referee orders a scrum and the put-in is given to the team that was moving forward immediately before the ruck stopped. If neither team was moving forward (or if the ref can't decide), then the put-in goes to the team that was moving forward immediately before the ruck began. Failing this, the attacking team gets the put-in. (The attacking team is always the team in its opponents' half of the field.)

Scrum after maul

This is more complicated. For one thing, a maul comes to an end *either* when the ball becomes unplayable *or* when the maul stops moving or collapses. That's when the referee must blow up and order a scrum. The team that puts in the ball is the team that did *not*

Bent arrows. When the ball fails to come out of a ruck or a maul, the referee orders a scrum. After a sterile ruck (ball on ground), the put-in goes to the team moving forward just before the ruck stopped. After a sterile maul (ball held), the team that took the ball into the maul loses the put-in to its opponents. A scrum from a maul resulting from a ball caught direct from an opponent's kick may be different: see text.

have the ball when the maul began. Use it or lose it. Sometimes the referee can't tell which team had it; in that case, the team moving forward before the maul came to a halt puts in the ball. If neither team was moving forward, the put-in goes to the attacking team.

There's more. A maul that forms after a player catches an opponent's kick-ahead may be a special case.

Suppose a player fields a kick-ahead, direct from his opponent's boot, and before he can move, players arrive and a maul forms. The maul goes nowhere or the ball fails to come out. The referee orders a scrum. In this case, the team of the player who originally caught the ball gets the put-in.

This exception does not apply to a ball caught from a kick-off or drop-out.

The front row

The front rows are the heart of a scrum. This is where it all happens. The rest is just horsepower.

Each front row must have three players in it – no more and no less. These three must link together firmly, so that they don't fall apart, and must combine properly with their opponents, so that nobody dislocates anything.

This means that the front rows must not form up some distance apart and charge each other. (An Irish forward actually broke his neck doing this in 1924.) And it means that the players must interlock naturally, with opposing heads next to each other. Two front-row players of the same team with their idiot heads locked together just break everything apart.

Within living memory, scrums collapsed, repeatedly. They no sooner assembled than they disintegrated. Throughout the land,

Opposing heads must alternate. The heads of the two front rows must interlock so that adjacent heads belong to opposing teams.

front-row forwards stuffed their faces into the mud, got up, heard the ref tell them not to do it again, and promptly did it again. And again. And again. Meanwhile, halfbacks and threequarters were being stretchered off with hypothermia.

That is why the scrum law now takes so much trouble over instructing front rows about staying on their feet.

For a start, the scrum-half should have the ball in his hands, ready to feed the scrum, before anyone thinks about making a tunnel. Then the two front rows should be standing not more than an arm's length apart, already crouched and in a position – when the referee calls 'Engage' – to meet. (If they're ready to meet. It's not an order. It's permission.) And when the front rows meet, each player must keep his head and shoulders no lower than his hips, thus ensuring that all six backbones are more or less horizontal.

The law about binding does two jobs. It keeps the front row intact, and it stops the hooker from swinging like a trapeze artist.

Every player in the front row must bind, and keep on binding, around his mate's body. The props latch on to their hooker, the hooker clamps both arms around his props. They must all bind around the body – *not* across the shoulders – so that they grip at or below armpit-level. If they do this properly, the scrum won't disintegrate and the hooker cannot swing into the middle of his opponents' second row.

The tunnel

The only reason for having the two front rows is to form a tunnel for putting the ball into, quickly and fairly. Therefore, like all good tunnels, this one must be open and dependable.

All front-row players must have their feet on the ground. Their feet must not be crossed, and they must be in a position to shove. That is what the law says. It doesn't say they have to shove, but it does say they have to be *in a position* to shove, and to shove forward.

A quick experiment against the nearest wall will prove that the only way to shove forward is to place the feet towards the rear. How far to the rear is a matter of taste, but an angle of forty-five degrees is one that appeals to many referees with long experience in the shoving business. Other referees feel that forty-three degrees is

**MIDDLE
LINE**

*Scrum-half's view of the tunnel. This shows (more or less) how the front-row
players must have their feet back and in a position to shove, so that the ball can be
put into the middle of the tunnel. Note that the left arm of the loosehead prop (black
shirt) must be either inside the tighthead prop's right arm or 'strutted' against his
own thigh. Note also the horizontal backs: spines in line.*

quite adequate, or that on a wet day forty-nine degrees is the
absolute minimum. It's all a bit academic, because the laws also say
that front-row players must keep their feet back far enough to allow
a clear tunnel, come rain or shine. So that clinches it. Keep your size
elevens pulled back so that the referee can see plenty of daylight on
the other side, and you'll be all right.

If all this makes the front row of a scrum sound as balanced and
sober as a Baptist missionary reunion, that is unfortunate, because
it doesn't work out that way. Veins bulge, joints crack, discs slip,
strange animal noises are heard, and – to paraphrase Dylan Thomas
– steam comes gushing out of their nostrils. Considerable heaving
and grinding take place.

Nevertheless, despite all the sado-masochism, the front rows
have a duty to keep the tunnel standing and open. The hooker, for
instance, must not hang entirely from his props: some of his weight
must always be on his own feet. The tighthead prop must bind on
his opposing loose-head prop by putting his right arm *outside* the
loose-head's arm and gripping his jersey, (not sleeve or arm). If the
loose-head prop wants to bind his opposing prop, his left arm must
be *inside* his opponent's right arm; if he doesn't want to bind, he

must put his left hand or forearm on his left thigh. (He can swap positions during the scrum, if he wants.) This alternative is available to help a loose-head prop to 'strut' himself when he's being given a hard time by a more powerful opponent – who, of course, has the advantage of being able to shove with both shoulders, while the loose-head prop can work with only one. And if all these detailed rulings strike you as being a bit longwinded, take it from me they're worth it. Their purpose is to avoid a lot of ill-tempered wrestling and some serious injuries too.

With each pack weighing well over half a ton, the pressure on the front rows is hefty enough already, without prop forwards trying to force their opponents' heads into the mud by dragging them down. A deliberately collapsed scrum is a temporary pain in the neck to other players, but it could be a permanent pain in the spine to a doubled-up prop.

A front-row player must not at any time – either before or after the ball is in – take both feet off the ground at once, or deliberately do anything else that might make the scrum collapse, such as twisting his body or forcing it downwards. Also once the ball is in the tunnel, he must not kick it back out again.

This is all pretty obvious. A scrum is to heel the ball. You can't have people deliberately preventing either the scrum or the heel from taking place.

The second and back rows

Time was (and not so very long ago) when any number of players could join in the scrum. The entire team could get down and shove, if they wished. But that's all been changed. Now the maximum (and minimum) is eight. All eight must bind. You are not in a scrum unless you have at least one hand and arm *around the body* of a team-mate. You don't have to shove, but you must keep a firm grip on his rib-cage. Resting your hand lightly on the small of his back is not binding, either legally or physically.

If you are a flanker, packing in a 3–4–1 formation, you must bind around the second row, not the prop. This goes back to the principle of a three-man front row. A flanker who attaches himself to a prop-forward is creating a *four*-man front row. Another thing: as long as the ball is in the tunnel, only the front-row players may play it. No poaching by the second row, or indeed any other player. (The flanker is usually the villain.) Not surprisingly, second- and back-row forwards must not do any of the things which front-row forwards are not allowed to do. They must not collapse the scrum, or deliberately fall down, and if the ball comes out of the scrum they must not put it back in. Nobody at all is allowed to handle the ball in a scrum, and that covers picking it up with your legs. (Why would anyone want to? Vanity? Boredom? Mental breakdown?)

Scrums: where?

You can have a scrum anywhere in the field-of-play – and nowhere else. So touch lines and goal lines are death to scrums.

The scrum should go down as near as possible to where the stoppage happened. If this is less than five metres from a touch line then the scrum is formed five metres from touch. This means there is a clear space five metres wide between the touch line and the scrum when it forms. If the mark is near a goal-line, the referee makes sure that the feet of all the defending players in the scrum are in the field-of-play when the scrum forms. Since all eight players are needed to form a scrum, this means the No. 8's feet must be in the field-of-play when the scrum-half puts in the ball.

The scrum must stay where it went down until the ball goes in, and it must be fairly square, too – not in shape but in position. The referee will make sure the tunnel is roughly parallel with the goal-lines when the scrum-half feeds it. He won't allow either pack to try to shove their opponents into the car park before that happens. The game restarts where it stopped. A team that heaves the scrum away from the mark before the ball can be put in will get penalised.

And now – for I see that the scrum-half has, at last, retrieved the ball from the sewage farm behind the pavilion – we might let him have a little go at throwing it into the tunnel.

Putting the ball in

This, it goes without saying, he should do honestly and fairly, so that both hookers get a good chance to hook the ball, and before we go any further I just want to say that if there is any more of that coarse, cynical laughter I shall go back to writing TV commercials. It's not my fault that all scrum-halves are cheats, rogues and con men. It must be something to do with their genes.

Mind you, the law as it is written doesn't leave the scrum-half much room for manoeuvre, although this hasn't noticeably stopped him trying. What it says is this:

The scrum-half must stand one metre from the scrum, on the middle line. (He may choose which side of the scrum to stand, but if he has any brains he'll put the ball in on his loose-head prop's side – normally the left. Having chosen, he must stick to it.) He must hold the ball in both hands, over the middle line, and midway between his knee and ankle. Then, *without dummying or moving the ball back,* he must put the ball quickly straight down the middle of the tunnel – that is, along a line where the opposing front rows' shoulders meet – so that it touches the ground just past the first prop-forward. So it must travel at least the width of the prop's shoulders into the scrum.

Photofit of a scrum-half at the put-in. Note that he holds the ball midway between the legs, and midway between knee and ankle. From here he puts it in straight, with one action (no backward movement, no dummying), so that it touches the ground beyond the nearer prop.

And until it leaves the scrum-half's hands, no front-row forward may raise a foot.

You would think that that spelt it all out clearly enough, wouldn't you? And yet getting the ball into the scrum has caused more problems that any other single aspect of the game. Players complain that no two referees apply the same interpretation. Referees complain that players don't follow the law. Spectators just complain, not that anyone cares about them.

If it's any consolation, life was always thus. Down through the years men have aged and withered under the strain of finding a better way to put the ball into the scrum. In 1920 New Zealand suggested that the referee should do the job. In 1929 the International Board thought scrum-halves were standing too far away and throwing too hard. In 1931 the law was changed to make the scrum-half 'gently propel' the ball in. That didn't work very well, and next year the IB warned against 'throwing the ball into the scrummage with unnecessary force'. In 1934 the Rugby Football Union was explaining that 'gently propel' now meant that 'the ball is not put in at excessive speed'. In 1937 the scrum-half was told to put the ball in 'fairly, at moderate speed'. That didn't work, either, and in 1939 an RFU committee suggested scrapping everything and just telling the scrum-half to stand a metre away and pitch the thing in, since that was what he was doing anyway.

Ulster wanted the speed to be 'slow' instead of 'moderate'. Wales, however, liked 'moderate'. Scotland ignored the speed question and asked for several other changes. Leinster, Munster and Connaught each had their own ideas, and so did Hitler.

Hitler's proposals held attention until 1946, when the entire scrum law was considerably tidied up. This worked quite well, and in 1947 a South African suggestion that the ball be *rolled* into the scrum got nowhere, thank God.

The law today says that the ball should be put in quickly, and if you want to know what that means, it means 'at a quick speed as distinct from a slow speed'; so you can see that things haven't changed all that much.

The best advice for any scrum-half is simply to try and look at things from the referee's point of view occasionally. What does the referee want? He wants the scrum-half to get on with it and put the ball in as soon as the scrum is ready. He wants him to put it in hard enough to get past the loose-head prop, but not so hard that it rockets out the other side.

He would *like* him to put it in fairly – straight down the middle line of the tunnel – but he will usually settle for having it put in not too unfairly. He might let you steal an inch or so, but if you try and shoot the ball under your hooker's feet *and* the referee's eye, he is likely to feel insulted. It all boils down to this: don't be greedy.

Hooking the ball; foot-up

The ball must go into the scrum fairly (or not too unfairly), and it must come out in a similar way.

By common consent the hooker is responsible for this, since the ball must pass the loose-head prop, and the hooker is the next man in line. But the law which governs the hooker's actions also applies to the rest of the front-row players.

The hooker must not strike until the ball has touched the ground. After that he can go for the ball with either foot, provided he doesn't take both feet off the ground at once.

You will recall that the scrum-half is under orders to put the ball in quickly. People have calculated that if he does, and if it goes where it should, and if the hooker does not strike too soon, then the whole thing is impossible because the ball will have flashed across his bows before he can get a foot to it, such being the laws of nature. Other people have proved the same thing with motion pictures of the ball beating the hooker comfortably and barely getting trapped by the far-side props as it makes its bid for freedom.

What they are getting at is that any hooker who actually hooks the ball first time must have struck too soon, and thus be guilty of foot-up. It may be so. Nevertheless, every week-end tens of thousands of hookers do manage to satisfy the referee *and* hook the ball, so there must be a way. What that way is, exactly, is something to be forged in the heat of battle; but a handy slice of advice for hookers is the same as the maxim for scrum-halves: don't be greedy.

Purists may consider that cynical, but then no purist was ever a hooker. Or *vice versa*.

A bad case of foot-up. This is what the scrum-half sees when his hooker, instead of letting the ball get right inside the tunnel, strikes too soon. Not a wise move.

Hookers tend to be the forgotten men of rugby, rather like miners, doing cramped and exhausting work where no one can see; so they might appreciate this small historical note, just to show that things could be worse. At least as late as 1889 the object of a scrum was not to hook the ball backwards but to hack it forwards, until you had kicked it right through your opponents. This might take some time – five minutes, ten? – because what with all the hacking going on, somebody was bound to miss the ball, and that might lead to deplorable retaliation, which in turn provoked more of the same, so that even when the ball did come out, views continued to be exchanged quite frankly and fearlessly in the depths of the meeting. Today's scrums have their share of crunch, but at least it's usually a short, sharp crunch.

Heeling the ball

One reason why the crunch is short and sharp is that it is now very easy to heel the ball from the scrum. It can come out anywhere except by the tunnel. You can heel the ball out between the prop's legs, or between the prop and the flanker, or through the flanker, or the second row – anywhere at all, as long as it's behind the tunnel.

The scrum-half can put the ball in and have it heeled out to him half a second later, only a couple of feet away.

If the ball comes back out of the tunnel, the same scrum-half puts it in again, and on the same side. This applies if it goes right through the tunnel. If no front-row player touches the ball, and the prop on the far side sticks out a foot so that the ball goes behind it, this is *not* heeling, and the ball gets put in again.

However, there's an interesting variation on this. It's the kind of thing that has specialists in the finer points of front-row play chuckling with delight, like tax accountants who've just discovered another loophole. It has to do with advantage.

The advantage law says that advantage does not apply when the ball comes out of the tunnel at either end, *not having been played*. Note carefully those last four words. They make all the difference. You cannot have an advantage (in law) unless somebody's done something wrong. Now, suppose the scrum-half feeds the ball into the scrum crookedly; that's an offence. But suppose the ball is then played by any of the front-row players (which side they're on doesn't matter) and suppose it then pops out of the tunnel, where a flanker (say) who is an opponent of the feeding scrum-half unbinds and snaps it up. The referee can play advantage and let him go.

Another example: the scrum-half feeds, and the opposing hooker strikes too soon. His foot kicks the ball back out of the tunnel and into the same scrum-half's hands, and the scrum-half runs with it. The referee's entitled to play advantage, because (1) somebody infringed and (2) the ball was played before (3) it came out of the tunnel.

If the ball is heeled back by the second row, the number eight forward can detach himself from the scrum and pick it up, even though it is in front of him. By breaking from the scrum, he has in fact placed the ball outside it.

Picking the ball out

Normally, of course, it's the scrum-half who does the snapping-up, and he does it only when the ball has come right out of the scrum. Handling the ball in the scrum, you will remember, is illegal, and that goes for the scrum-half as much as the forwards. If his forwards

Ball in, ball out. In (A) the ball is still in the scrum, so the scrum-half must not handle it. In (B) the No. 8 has moved his right foot up, so that the ball is now out and the scrum-half can legally pick it up.

heel the ball with all the free-flowing ease of cold treacle, that's just too bad: he'll have to wait for it. Even if it's lying right between his number eight's feet, within easy reach, the scrum-half must let it come to him, and not go in after it.

There is an easy test to decide whether or not a scrum-half is picking the ball out of a scrum. You say to yourself: if the ball were left where it is, and if an opponent were to come thundering round the scrum, would he be offside? If the answer is yes, then the ball is still in the scrum.

Not every scrum-half thinks this way. A good few feel that the ball is in the scrum until such time as they pick it out. It's an attractive theory, if you're a scrum-half, but not if you're an opponent – or a referee.

Scrum offside

There are two separate offside laws for scrums. One applies only to the scrum-halves. The other applies to everyone else.

Scrum-half offside

For scrum-halves, the offside line runs through the ball itself. As long as the ball is in the scrum, each scrum-half must stay on his own side of it.

This can make life a bit difficult for the scrum-half whose side *has not* heeled the ball. There he is, edging his way around the perimeter of the pack, trying to stay onside and yet also trying to get close enough to pounce when his opposite number grabs the ball. If he is too eager he will overstep the ball while it is still in the scrum; if he is too cautious it will pop out while he's out of range. He has to walk the fine line between giving away a penalty kick and giving away possession.

This assumes that the ball is heeled quickly, something which last happened in November 1937. When the ball comes back slowly, the scrum-half on the non-heeling side has more time in which to follow it through. However, even if he can see it, he must not try to kick it out of the scrum.

Both scrum-halves are forbidden to kick the ball while it's still in the scrum. What's more, the scrum-half who *didn't* put the ball in is not allowed to circle around to the *opposite* side of the scrum and patrol that area. On that side, he can go no further than the rest of his backs – which means staying behind the tail-end of the scrum, until the ball is out.

Not so the scrum-half who put the ball into the scrum, though. He is free to stroll around to the opposite side whenever he likes (provided, of course, he stays behind the ball in the scrum). And if his forwards are skilled enough to channel the ball out through the south-east corner of the scrum, there's precious little the opposing scrum-half can do to prevent him from snapping it up and putting it to work, what with that back row shielding him like a set of flying

OFF-SIDE
LINE
FOR
SCRUM-HALVES

OFF-SIDE LINE
FOR BACKS

Scrum offside lines. While the ball is in the scrum, each scrum-half must stay on his own side of the ball. All other players (normally the backs) must stay behind the tail-end of the scrum until the ball comes out.

buttresses. It all means that any pack of forwards which is good enough to hook the ball and heel it intelligently can pretty well guarantee their scrum-half perfect possession.

What's more the scrum-half whose team wins the ball is granted one small advantage by the law. When the ball is still in the scrum, he can plant one foot in front of it without being offside. (This is to help him get his pass away.) The opposing scrum-half must keep *both* his feet behind the ball, or he's offside.

'Offside trap' banned

One thing a scrum-half must not do is try to lure his opponents offside. In the past this has been the cause of much bad acting. While the ball was held in his back row, the scrum-half would exercise his arms, as if passing to his outside-half. It's now illegal for a scrum-half to do anything to make his opponents think the ball is out of the scrum when it's not. The offside trap is dead.

Offside for the rest

For everyone except the scrum-halves, the scrum offside line runs through the tail-end of their side of the scrum. (Thus there are *two* offside lines, one for each team.) Normally, when the scrum forms properly, the line runs through the feet of the number eight forward, since these stick out furthest. Until the scrum ends every player who is not part of the scrum must keep both feet behind this line (or behind his goal line, if the scrum is straddling it). The scrum ends when the ball is heeled out, so the side which gets the ball starts off with anything up to ten or twelve feet of clear ground between it and the nearest tackler (except for the opposing scrum-half)– enough space to start an attack.

This is what the law wants to happen. Its aim is to nail the back row to the scrum until the ball comes out – the only exception being the hindmost player (usually the No. 8), who can unbind from the scrum if he has the ball at his feet. But neither the No. 8 nor the flankers, at either end of the scrum, are allowed to break away early. The back rows must bind and remain bound until the ball is out. If a team wins possession in a scrum, its flankers or No. 8 can no longer detach themselves in readiness for a back-row attack. Similarly, the opposing team cannot detach its back row to form a defensive barrier. The glory days of the marauding back row are gone.

This is nothing new. The lawmakers have been balancing attack with defence ever since the game began. Fifty years ago, the off-side line at scrums ran though the ball; and so it moved with the ball in the scrum. Wing forwards (as flankers were known then) could break and follow the ball as it got heeled through their opponents' scrum, until they were poised, itching to pounce on the scrum-half. If he avoided their clutches, the outside-half got the ball with little space to work in.

Life wasn't much easier at line-outs. The offside line ran down the line-of-touch, which meant that it was possible for the opposing three quarters to stand toe-to-toe. With no maximum length for the line-out, wing forwards were free to roam and cause

You get only one referee at a match. You can make the best of him, or you can make the worst of him – but you won't change him. If you cause him problems, he's likely to pay more attention to you than to your opponents who are not causing him problems. Is that going to help you win the game? Moral: Think what you like, but keep your big mouth shut.

havoc in midfield. The wonder is that halfbacks and centres ever had a chance.

Eventually, the lawmakers restored some balance. Offside lines got pushed back to the hindmost foot at the scrum (and ruck, and maul) and to a line ten metres behind the line-out. The second rows were obliged to remain bound to the scrum. (Within living memory, only the front row was necessary to form a scrum, and it was not unknown for a captain with a weak scrum to pull out his back five and tell them to go off and tackle somebody.) The changed laws created space for the team that won the ball: twenty metres of it at a line-out; three metres or more at a scrum.

For a while, the balance was good. Then, gradually, three things happened. First, back-row players got fitter and faster. They made space shrink. Secondly, they stopped even pretending to shove when it was the opposition's put-in at the scrum; instead they broke off and plugged a few gaps in defence. And thirdly, coaches got better at coaching defence rather than attack. As a result of all this, the midfield became crowded with players once more. Attacks were stifled. The balance was lost again.

Hence the lawmakers' introduction of an eight-man scrum bound solid until it ends. This makes a difference three ways. The team winning possession should be able to get the ball back and out fast, before the opposition can use an eight-man shove to disrupt the heel. With the opposing flankers pinned to the scrum, the half-backs should have more time to make their moves. And with the No. 8 a fixture at each end, the scrum becomes a yard or two longer – which widens the gap between the offside lines and thereby creates more space for attack.

And in case you're wondering what happens when a team is down to fewer than fifteen players because of injury or sending-off, they're allowed to reduce their number in the scrum accordingly.

When the scrum turns: the 90-degree law

Once upon a time, back in the days when all decent rugby shorts reached the knee and well-bred scrum-halves wore mitts, there was a referee's nightmare called The Rotating Scrum.

What happened was the scrum wheeled until it had made a half-circle. The scrum offside lines were supposed to run through the tail-ends of the scrum, but now the tails had become the heads. What if a flanker were to break? Which way should he run to get onside? Forward or back? Who could go where? And why?

At this point the referee usually awoke, bathed in a cold sweat.

All that, thank God, is a thing of the past. If a scrum is wheeled through more than 90 degrees (a quarter circle), so that the middle line – the line of the scrum-half's feed – has moved beyond a position parallel with the touch lines, then the referee calls a halt, blows up, and re-sets the scrum. He does this at the place where the old scrum ended (which may be some distance from where it began). Whichever team had won possession in the old scrum, that team puts in the ball at the new one. If neither team had won possession, the put-in stays with the team that previously had it.

90-degree wheels seem to arrive in clusters, like meteorites or buses. Meanwhile no rugby gets played. That's when the referee is liable to point out that any team which intentionally wheels the scrum 90 degrees or more is guilty of Unfair Play, and there are penalties for this. Sanity soon prevails.

As for players not in the scrum: wheeling changes nothing. Scrum-halves must stay behind the ball, and other backs must stay behind their tail-end of the scrum. As the scrum rotates, that tail-end might no longer belong to their No 8. It might conceivably attach to a lock, or even a prop. Makes no difference. The offside line runs through the hindmost foot. That's the law.

Penalties for scrum offences

Wrongdoing in or around a scrum is penalised *either* by a penalty kick *or* by a free kick.

The free-kick offences are for what you might call 'technical mistakes'– crooked feed; hooker striking too soon; front-row feet blocking the tunnel; kicking the ball out of the tunnel; putting the ball back in the scrum; any delay; working the offside trap; and so on. It's also a free-kick offence if a team shoves the scrum off the mark before the ball is in.

Scrum-linked crimes that lead to penalty kicks are the more serious things – one front row charging another; any player binding illegally; 'popping' an opponent; twisting or dipping so as to collapse a scrum; handling the ball in a scrum; flanker widening his angle to obstruct opposing scrum-half; and all sorts of offside.

These are all a threat to the player or the game, or both. Interesting to note that the law book devotes three pages to describing how the front rows should bind, but only three lines to how the rest of the scrum should bind. If a flanker can't bind, the scrum won't fall down. If a prop slips his binding, it might. That's why props have to be far more intelligent than flankers. I know. I was one.

Readers write

M.F. of Cork writes: I never heard such fairytales as that stuff you wrote about scrums.

D.R. Give me an example.

M.F. For a start, the scrum-half never stands one metre from the scrum, he always stands closer. And he always feeds his own hooker, and the hooker is never in a position to shove. If his props were to let go of him, he'd fall down sideways! Don't you ever watch TV?

D.R. Anything else?

M.F. Front-row players never bind around the armpits. Most of them haven't got arms long enough. And their shoulders are usually lower than their hips. Every prop tries to pull his opponent down. It's a private battle up front, isn't it? Who needs laws?

D.R. The players need them because sometimes everything goes to hell, the ball never gets into the tunnel, the scrum keeps collapsing, and so on. Players get hurt. That's when the referee uses the laws to rebuild the scrum from scratch. And he needs laws to stop players cheating. For instance, a hooker who slips his binding is getting an unfair advantage, because he can strike further and faster.

* * *

T.W. of Queensland writes: When is the ball out of the scrum? I've seen it lying in the same spot for a long time before the scrum-half picked it up. If it was out, why didn't the other scrum-half go for it?

D.R. I've often asked myself that question.

* * *

D.S.K. of Harrow writes: This is about the scrum-half who didn't put in the ball. What's to stop him running wide, ready to tackle the centres? If he stays behind the ball, he's onside.

D.R. The lawmakers thought of that one. They ruled that the scrum-half must either stay near the scrum or get behind his scrum's offside line.

8
Rucks and mauls

A ruck
Puts the ball in the muck,
Whereas a maul
Requires hands on the ball. *

Rucks

If you have thoroughly read and completely understood all the preceding guff about scrums – all right, don't lie to me – you won't have any trouble understanding rucks.

A ruck is simply a scrum with all the starch taken out of it. Its purpose is the same – to get the ball back in play – and most of the laws that cover a scrum apply to a ruck.

The big difference, of course, is that you can't have any specialists in a ruck, which is simply a first-up, first-down affair. This cuts out all the scrum-half/hooker/flanker/number eight rubbish, because none of those gents is recognisable in a ruck. And we are spared the pomp and ceremony of putting the ball in, since the ball is already in. This effectively eliminates any special scrum-half offside law, because after all *any* player could be scrum-half at a ruck, so no favoured treatment is going to be handed out there. There is only one offside law for rucks, and it applies to everybody.

* Anonymous Japanese haiku.

What is a ruck?

First things first, however. What exactly is a ruck? It's important to know this, because you are not, for instance, allowed to handle the ball in a ruck. On the other hand, if you hesitate to grab the thing because you aren't sure whether or not a ruck is taking place, you could be missing a slice of glory. So pay close attention.

To have a ruck, all you need is one player from each team in the field-of-play, on their feet and shoving each other, with the ball on the ground between them.

If any other player joins the ruck, he must bind on to a team-mate; but the heart of a ruck is simply a pair of opponents, shoving over the ball on the ground. If they are not opponents, or if they're not shoving each other, or if the ball is not on the ground, or if it's on the ground but not between them, then it's not a ruck, and you can go where you like and do what you will (subject to the other laws, of course).

What makes a ruck. This get-together meets all the requirements of a ruck: ball on the ground, in the field-of-play, with opponents over it and shoving each other. The offside lines run through the tail-ends of a ruck. You must either join it, from behind your own offside line, or get behind it. If you join it, you must do so alongside the hindmost player – not in front of him. You're not in a ruck unless you're bound onto it. Shoulders must be no lower than hips.

Offside at a ruck

The ruck offside lines run through the tail-ends of the ruck, just as they do in scrums. If you are not in a ruck you have a choice. You can *either* get behind its tail-end (if you're not already there) and stay behind it, *or* you can join the ruck. If you want to join it, you've got to start from your team's side of it. Then find your hindmost team-mate in the ruck and get stuck in alongside him or behind him. Do not join the ruck in front of him, or you'll be offside.

This is important. Often there is an attractive opening halfway up the side of the ruck, just tailormade for you to slot into. Don't be seduced. The laws says that anyone joining a ruck must add himself to the tail. Same applies if you leave a ruck. First, you get behind your offside line, and do it fast. Then, if you want to rejoin, attach yourself to the nearest team-mate at the stern. The ball may be elsewhere. It may be very elsewhere. Forget it.

If you're not in the ruck, stay behind the offside line until the ruck ends, which is when the ball comes out.

Rucks tend to take place unexpectedly, of course. It is not uncommon for a whole slew of players to be caught offside when a ruck suddenly breaks out. Nor will they suffer for it, necessarily. Provided they don't hang around, and provided they do their little best to scurry back where they belong, the referee will look upon them charitably. It is when he sees them shambling back, and notes that they are not displaying that bustle and vigour of ten minutes ago when they thought they were going to score a try for the first time in twelve years – *that* is when he gets impatient and starts handing out penalty kicks.

When you come to think of it, there is precious little point in ruck-mooching and risking getting caught for being offside. If you're going to get stuck into a ruck, you might as well pull your finger out and *do* it. If you're not, then you might as well prepare to make yourself useful when the ball comes out. If it comes out on your side, you'd better be behind it, for obvious reasons. It *might* come out on *their* side, of course. On the other hand, it might not. If it doesn't, and you are still hanging about offside, you'll be perfectly positioned to do sweet nothing. Can this be good?

There are various other things to say about rucks – things like:

don't handle the ball in a ruck; don't make the ruck collapse; don't jump on a ruck; don't fake a pass from a ruck – the Offside Trap is banned at rucks as well as scrums; if you're on the ground get away from the ball … but you know all that stuff by now anyway.

In any case, it's all common sense. As we said before, a scrum is to heel the ball away. You can't have people deliberately preventing either the scrum or the heel from taking place – and that applies to rucks too. Much scoring comes after rucks, so every player should understand them. That means backs as well as forwards. There is no class discrimination at the bottom of the heap.

Mauls

The big difference between a ruck and a maul – listen, because I'm not going to say this again – is that for a ruck the ball must be on the ground, whereas for a maul a ball must be carried. *A ruck needs only two players, whereas a maul must have at least three: one from each side around the man who is carrying the ball, in the field-of-play, and all of them*

What makes a maul. A maul is like a ruck except that the ball is held, not on the ground. It needs at least one player from each team plus the man with the ball, all caught up in the maul or bound onto it. The offside lines run through the tail-ends. You either join the maul (from behind your offside line) or you get behind it. You must join alongside the hindmost player, not in front of him.

Ruck and maul offside. This handy all-purpose illustration could be a ruck (ball on ground) or a maul (ball held). Offside is the same for both. The offside lines run through the tail-ends of the ruck or maul (through the hindmost foot). Any player in front of his team's offside line must get behind it, fast, or he may be penalised for loitering with intent to spoil his opponents' possession. The player marked with a cross is loitering. He's in trouble.

wrestling for possession. You are not in a maul unless you're caught up in the struggle or bound on to it.

Maul offside

The offside law for mauls follows the same lines as scrum and ruck offside. The offside lines at a maul run through the tail-ends of the maul. And – just as with a ruck – you have a choice. You can *either* get behind the maul and stay there until it ends, *or* you can join it. If

Leaving and rejoining a ruck or maul. This overhead view shows a ruck or maul. The offside law is the same for both. A player in a ruck or maul who wants to leave it must first get back behind his team's offside line. This runs through the tail-end. Then he can rejoin it, provided he does so alongside the hindmost player – not in front of him.

you join it, do so alongside or behind your hindmost team-mate in the maul. If you want to pull out and rejoin it, unplug yourself and retire behind your offside line first; then plug in alongside or behind your hindmost team-mate, but not in front of him. All very familiar, isn't it?

I said a lot about players who get caught in an offside position when a ruck breaks out and then get into hot water for loitering. Exactly the same applies to mauls. So does the banned Offside Trap. Faking a pass from a maul is illegal.

Loitering on the wing

When someone gets done for loitering at a ruck or maul it's usually a forward, caught hanging about on the wrong side of the offside line. Sometimes it's a centre who has crept too far forward. But you don't often see a wing-threequarter being penalised. After all, he's so far from the action – perhaps 50 or 60 metres – what difference does it make if he's a step or three in front of the tail-end of a ruck or maul on the other side of the field?

Ask his opponents. If they win possession, move the ball wide, and suddenly see the enemy winger closing down their options, it's because he had an unfair start on them. (Referees call this 'The Banana Effect' – when the wing is offside he's in front of his centres, and the backline curves like a banana.) Thus an offside player loitering on the wing can be as damaging to an attack as if he were loitering on the fringe of the ruck or maul. By cutting down his opponents' options, he's damaging their chances of attack. The offside line stretches from touch line to touch line, and there's a good reason for that.

Scrum after ruck or maul

I know we did all this in the chapter on scrums, but a quick round-up would do no harm.

When the ball in a ruck is unplayable, the put-in at the scrum goes to the team that was moving forward just before the ruck stopped. Failing that, it goes to the team moving forward just before the ruck began; and failing *that*, to the attacking team (the team in its opponents' half).

When the ball in a maul becomes unplayable, or when the maul stops moving, the put-in at the scrum goes to the team that was *not* in possession of the ball when the maul began. If the ref can't decide, then the team last moving forward gets the put-in; failing that, it goes to the attacking team. The put-in following a maul after a kick-ahead has been caught may be different.

So, here's a summary of the round-up. After a ruck, the team finally moving forward gets the put-in. After a maul, the team originally in possession does *not* get the put-in. They didn't use it, so they lose it. Makes you think.

The pile-up

After scrums, rucks and mauls, there is a fourth type of steaming heap to be seen on the rugby field. It's known as a pile-up. You won't find the word anywhere in the lawbook, but every referee knows what it looks like; so we might as well cover it here.

Rucks and mauls have this in common: the players are on their feet. Sometimes the irresistible force hits the immovable object, and the object moves. The feet lose their footing. Civilisation crumbles. Next thing you know, bodies are stacked horizontally like logs of wood. What is the referee to make of this? It's not a ruck, nor a maul. It's a pile-up.

If he reckons the ball will pop out fairly immediately, he might give it a brief chance. If it doesn't, he must blow up and order a scrum. However, he has a couple of other shots in his locker. If he reckons a player is lying on or near the ball when he could get away if he tried, the referee can penalise him. If he reckons a player intentionally fell on or over the pile-up, thus making the ball even more unplayable, he can penalise him.

The referee should not delay. Because the pile-up is a helpless mess, there's a big risk someone might make it even worse with his boot. The pile-up is a clot in the bloodstream of the game, and the referee has a powerful de-clotting agent: his whistle.

Readers write

P.N. of Manchester writes: I saw a bloke convert a try by standing with his back to the posts and drop-kicking the ball over the bar with his heel. Brilliant!

D.R. What's that got to do with rucks and mauls?

P.N. Nothing. My point is, the ref disallowed it. Why?

D.R. Because it wasn't a legal kick. The laws of the game say a kick means hitting the ball with your foot or leg, anywhere between the knee and the toe but not the heel. Back-heeling the ball over the bar is a fancy trick that scores *nul points*.

* * *

C.G. of Natal writes: Let's get this straight. Handling the ball in a ruck is wrong, but the scrum-half can use his foot to winkle it out of the edge of a ruck. Yes?

D.R. Yes. But if he sticks his foot in front of the ball in a ruck, and he's not binding on the ruck, he's offside.

C.G. What if he uses his hands to drag the ball out?

D.R. Unwise. You can't handle the ball in a ruck.

C.G. But the scrum-half can reach into a maul to get the ball.

D.R. Of course. The ball's being handled in a maul, anyway.

C.G. Can he put his foot into a maul?

D.R. Are you crazy? He'll pull a hamstring.

* * *

P. de B. of Paris writes: Quelle est la raison de la décision du 'put-in' dans la mêlée aprés un "maul" abortif, par contraste avec un 'ruck' abortif?

D.R. C'est simple. Parce que le ballon est par terre pendant un 'ruck', aucune équipe ne peut l'avoir en sa possession. Alors, l'equipe qui avance au début, merite le 'put-in'. Mais, pour faire un 'maul', un joueur doit avoir le ballon dans les mains. Donc, l'arbitre pense: 'Fais-en quelquechose, ou perds-le!' Si cette equipe ne peut pas recycler le ballon, le 'put-in' est donné à leurs adversaires - comme il se doit.

T.F. of Bradford writes: What was all that about?

D.R. The reasoning behind different put-ins at scrums after rucks and after mauls. A player actually carries the ball into a maul, so it's reckoned to be his team's fault if they can't get it out again. That's why they lose the put-in. But neither team possesses the ball when a ruck forms (ball on ground), so if it doesn't emerge, the team going forward before it stopped deserves to get the put-in.

* * *

H.A. of Cambridge writes: At a kick-off or a drop-out, the team receiving the kick often catch the ball and immediately bind onto the catcher and form a wedge. That's not a maul, is it?

D.R. No. A maul must have an opponent in it.

H.A. So there's no maul offside line, then.

D.R. Correct.

D.R. And any player on the kicker's team can legally go around the wedge and grab the ball.

D.R. He'd be a brave man. But you're right. If the kicker's team don't want to create a maul, then no maul exists, and their players are free to go anywhere.

* * *

A. McL. of Kelso writes: If the pile-up is so frequent, why isn't it in the laws?

D.R. I sometimes wonder that myself.

* * *

N.J.M. of Dorset writes: What if the ball-carrier in a maul goes to ground? Falls to his knees, for instance. It's not a ruck, but it's not a maul either – the ball-carrier should be on his feet in a maul. What next?

D.R. Unless the referee sees that the ball is likely to come out at once, he blows up and orders a scrum.

9

The law that nobody knows

Offside and onside following a quick ruck, maul, scrum or line-out

Nobody knows? I exaggerate. At the last count, four people did actually know this law: two referees, a sportswriter who has since left the country, and myself.

You may remember that earlier we said that in open play – not during scrums, rucks, mauls or line-outs – you could be offside only if you were in front of someone on your team who had the ball, or who played it last. That is what we said and we make no apology for it, because it's true – 99.9 per cent of the time.

There is just one situation, however, in which it isn't true. You can be offside, *even though your opponents have the ball and no scrum, ruck, maul or line-out is taking place,* if they have just forced a snap scrum, ruck, maul or line-out between you and your line, won the ball and started an attacking movement. In that situation you are offside and there's nothing you can legally do until they have put you onside, which they can do only by kicking the ball or running five metres with it. Passing the ball does *not* put you onside, not after they've forced a snap action and won quick possession from it. Understand?

No. As I thought. From the rows of sagging jaws, glassy eyeballs, and calloused thumbs scratching numbed skulls, I can see that we have achieved something less than total, blinding comprehension. Perhaps we should try it again, this time more slowly.

For a start, let's narrow it down to rucks and mauls. I suppose it's conceivable that this law might apply to a scrum or a line-out, but it's highly unlikely because everything would depend on a player taking so long to catch up with play that the scrum or the line-out could begin and end while he was still trying to get back to it. Possible, but very improbable. Rucks and mauls, on the other hand, are much more spontaneous affairs. It's not unusual for a player to find himself a long way on the wrong side of (say) a ruck. While he's running towards it, his opponents win the ruck and start passing the ball. He's offside, and nothing he does can change that. Only his opponents can put him onside, by kicking or by running five metres with the ball – not by passing it.

Picture this. Blues are playing Whites, and all the action is inside the Blues' half. Suddenly, a Blue player breaks clear and puts in a tremendous kick ahead. The Blue team races upfield and catches the White full-back in possession. A maul forms. Blues win the ball, get it out and start an attacking movement.

At this point some White defenders arrive on the scene, pounding back to help save the day. Obviously they *were* offside during the quick maul, but the maul is now over. On the other hand, would it be fair to let them rush into the game and destroy the Blue

Act One: The big Blue breakaway. A White attack fizzles out in the Blue half. Blues win the ball and a Blue player puts in a huge kick, deep into the White half.

Act Two: Blues beat Whites to the maul. The White full-back fields the kick. Blue players arrive, tackle him and force a maul. White defence is slow getting back.

attack? An attack which the Blue players sweated for and earned by being faster and more quick-thinking than Whites?

Wouldn't it be like rewarding Whites for being slower, and might it not be an incentive against hurrying back to join the maul or at least to get behind it where they're onside? After all, if the leisurely defender can turn up and immediately tackle an attacker, he might deliberately take his time, reckoning that Blues are going to win the ball anyway, and he can do more damage if he catches them starting an attack and tackles from behind than if he hurries and gets in front, where they can see him.

Clearly, slow play cannot be allowed to succeed at the expense of fast play. So the sluggish defender is made to pay for being late. An offside defender retiring towards a ruck or maul is covered by the appropriate offside law while the ruck or maul is going on. But, if his opponents have won the ball, and he's still slogging back, he's covered by the Forgotten Law of offside, which says he must not interfere with play until he's been put onside.

Only his opponents can do this. There is no offside line for him to retire behind. The only way he can become onside is for an opponent to kick the ball, or run five metres with it. Until then, the defender can only wait and curse, and he'd better do *that* under his breath.

In general play, a player is always put onside the moment an opponent plays the ball; for instance, by passing it. But this is not general play; it's a sort of untidy aftermath; and the leaden defenders don't get let off so easily. They must concede their opponents at least a run of five metres or a kick before they can interfere. A pass alone is not enough to put them onside; neither is two passes, nor three nor four. Only a kick or a five-metre run will do the trick.

The situation outlined above (Blues versus Whites) doesn't often happen. There isn't usually such a great difference in speed and stamina between the attacking and the defending sides. But there is

Act Three: Blues attack, Whites arrive, offside! Blues win quick possession and pass the ball. As they attack, White defenders arrive. They are offside. They must not take part in the game – even though the maul is over – until a Blue player kicks or runs 5 metres with the ball. This puts them onside. Nothing else does.

one aspect of the modern game where this particular offside law does increasingly apply, and that's the quick heel from a ruck following a scrum or line-out.

Say that Blues heel from a scrum and the ball reaches their fly-half, who gains fifteen metres and is tackled. Immediately, the Blue back-row zeroes in and rucks for the ball. They heel it out and are ready to start another passing movement when the White forwards arrive on the scene, too late to ruck but eager to tackle – and all offside.

Now, the ruck (or maul) is an important part of the game. Fast second-phase possession is the best way to revive an attack, when the defence has been sucked in by the ruck (or some of it, anyway).

Knowing this, a couple of the defending forwards may decide to take their time about covering across the field after a set piece, on the principle that the best time to reach a ruck is just after your opponents have heeled from it. Which is true as far as it goes. It just doesn't take into account the basic nature of the game. Rugby is meant to be a fast-moving, attacking game, and the Forgotten Law

First Phase: scrum ball – stand-off break – tackle. From a scrum, the Blue stand-off gains 20 metres and is tackled. The Blue back row, backing up fast, reach him and ruck. White forwards are just leaving the scrum.

PHASE
1

Second Phase: ruck ball – attack – defenders arrive – offside! Blues win the ruck ball quickly. White defenders reach the scene just as the Blues are beginning a passing movement. Whites are offside and must not interfere – even though the ruck is over – until a Blue player kicks or runs 5 metres with the ball. This puts them onside. Nothing else does.

QUICK POSSESSION FROM RUCK

ALL OFF-SIDE !

PHASE 2

of offside exists to protect that aim. It is very seldom applied, but it's always there, if needed.

It was needed in the England-New Zealand match of 1993. England suddenly broke out of their half and took play deep into the visitors' half. Just as England heeled the ball from a ruck, Sean Fitzpatrick (the All Black captain) arrived. The ruck was over. He knew he was still offside – his hands were raised in that familiar (but futile) gesture. He touched nobody, but he got in the way of the England scrum-half. And he got penalised for it.

Maybe more people know the law that nobody knows than I give credit for.

Readers write

L.G. of Chipping Sodbury writes: I've read that chapter three times and I still don't understand it.

D.R. Are you complaining or boasting?

10
Touch, and the throw-in

Touch

Where is it? Touch is the area beyond the sides of the field-of-play, and there's not much more to be said.

Two things save touch from being a complete waste of time. One, it provides somewhere for spectators to stand. Two, it marks a definite boundary to the field-of-play, without which everybody would be on the point of collapse after about four minutes.

Once the ball goes into touch it becomes dead, and play is restarted by throwing the ball in. The touch line is in touch, but the corner-posts are not – they are in touch-in-goal, which is a different story.

The ball alone. When the ball is in free flight (not held by a player) and it touches a touch line, or the ground (or anything on the ground) beyond the touch line, then the ball is in touch.

Note that being in touch is *not* a matter of crossing the touch line; it's a matter of landing on or beyond the touch line. If the ball flies through the air and crosses the touch line but swings back or gets blown back and comes down in the playing area, play goes on.

The ball carried. When a player is holding the ball and he touches a touch line or the ground beyond it, then the ball is in touch. Similarly, when the ball held by him touches a touch line or the ground beyond it, it's in touch.

But note the word 'ground'. If a tackler sweeps his opponent off his feet so that the tackler ends up in touch but he is *underneath* his opponent's legs, while the upper half is still in the playing area and still holding the ball – that ball is not in touch. The ball-carrier's feet and legs are over the touch line *but they haven't touched the ground*. If he can reach the goal line, he can score a try. Rory Underwood did exactly that when playing for England. All credit to the touch judge for knowing his law.

So it's contact with the ground on or beyond the touch line that matters. Let's assume the player himself is not in touch. If the player carrying the ball holds it over the touch line, it's not in touch. If it falls out of the sky beyond the touch line and he catches it without putting his feet on or over the touch line, it's not in touch. The same applies to touch-in-goal. He doesn't even have to catch the ball: he can reach across the touch line (or the touch-in-goal line) and knock it into the playing area, as long as he doesn't knock it forward. Or he can leap into the air and knock the ball inwards while his feet are off the ground, provided his leap began in the playing area.

Indeed, even stranger things are possible. If the player is in

Beyond touch isn't necessarily in touch. For the ball-carrier to be in touch, his body or the ball must touch the touch line or the ground beyond the touch line. If the ball-carrier is tackled and the tackler ends up in touch underneath the ball-carrier, then the ball-carrier has not touched the ground. He's not in touch. He can score a try. It's happened.

Out may still be in. The ball is not in touch just because it's falling beyond the touch line. If a player who has both feet in the field-of-play catches the ball, the ball is not in touch. Alternatively, he can knock the ball in-field. If he jumps and catches the ball, it is not in touch provided, when he lands, his feet are in the playing area.

touch, but the ball is not, he can legally reach across the touch line and hit the ball with his hand, or he can kick it, and it won't be in touch.

If he grabs it, of course, it will.

Remember always: the touch line itself is in touch. If the ball (or your boot if you're holding the ball) so much as brushes the chalk, then it's in touch.

That makes it dead. The throw-in brings it back to life again.

The throw-in

Where is the ball thrown in?

The question, you may have spotted, is not 'Where is the line-out held?' That too is a good question, and we'll get round to it soon. But when the ball goes into touch, a line-out is not always essential to get it back in play. You can have a throw-in without a line-out; so let's first sort out what the law has to say about throw-ins. The key phrase is 'gain in ground'.

Rugby is basically a game of handling and running. Agreed, there are moments when you have no choice but to bang the ball into touch, but the laws discourage unlimited touch-kicking.

PENALTY KICK ANYWHERE

THROW-IN HERE

THROW-IN HERE

ANY INDIRECT KICK ANYWHERE

22 M

THROW-IN HERE

ANY KICK FROM OWN 22 OR IN-GOAL

GOAL LINE

When touch-kicking gains ground. From the bottom upwards: When a player inside his 22 or in-goal kicks directly to touch, he gains ground. This also covers a free kick awarded inside the 22. If he kicks indirectly to touch (ball bounces in the field-of-play) there may be a gain in ground. When a player takes a penalty kick anywhere and kicks directly or indirectly to touch, there can be a gain in ground, and his team takes the throw-in.

It boils down to this. Outside your own 22, if you kick directly into touch – that is, if the ball doesn't touch the ground or another player before it goes out – then your kick gains no ground for your side: the ball is thrown in opposite the place where you kicked, not at the place where it went out. Inside your own 22 or your in-goal, you may kick directly into touch and still gain ground, provided you personally didn't take the ball into the 22. If you carry or knock

THROW-IN HERE

ANY DIRECT KICK (EXCEPT PENALTY KICK)

THROW-IN HERE

ANY FREE KICK TAKEN OUTSIDE 22

22 M

THROW-IN HERE

TAKES BALL INTO 22 AND KICKS DIRECT

GOAL LINE

When touch-kicking gains no ground. From the bottom upwards: When a player takes or puts the ball into his 22 and then kicks directly to touch, he gains no ground. Outside the 22, any free kick taken directly to touch gains no ground. Any kick (except a penalty kick) taken outside the 22 that goes directly to touch, gains no ground.

or kick the ball into your 22 and then you kick directly to touch, there's no gain in ground.

The only exception to this is penalty kicks. From anywhere on the field, a penalty kick into touch can result in a gain in ground, because the ball is thrown in at the place where it went out. This applies whether the penalty kick went directly into touch (on the full) or it went indirectly into touch (bounced first in the field-of-play). What's more, the kicker's team always gets the throw-in after a penalty kick to touch.

Free kicks are not an exception. Outside your 22, if you bang a free kick directly into touch, you gain no ground. Inside your 22, it's different; a free kick can gain ground just like any other kick – with one proviso. The free kick must have been *awarded inside* the 22. If your free kick is awarded *outside* your 22, you're entitled to take the kick as far behind the mark as you like; but if you cross your 22-metre line and then hoof that free kick directly to touch, you gain no ground. The throw-in will be opposite the place where you kicked.

What's going on? I'll tell you what's going on. The lawmakers want to discourage a team that's been given a free kick in midfield from retreating into their 22 in order to kick for touch. This was slowing down the game. The entire kicking team had to run back so that one man could boot the ball. Then they all ran forward again, for the throw-in. Tedious.

Naturally, any touch-kick which bounces in the field-of-play, or any grub-kick which goes into touch, gains ground for the kicker's side. The ball is thrown in where it crossed the touch-line. And that applies if the ball touches an opponent, too. It's a direct kick to touch only if the ball touches nothing at all on its way.

If you kick directly to touch and actually find touch behind you, then that's where the ball is thrown in, not opposite where you kicked. You get the worst of the deal, whatever it is. And if, from a kick-off, you kick the ball directly into touch, your opponents can (if they wish) take a line-out opposite the place where you kicked, i.e. on the halfway line. Similarly, at a 22 drop-out, if the kick goes directly into touch, the other team can (if they wish) take a line-out where the ball went out. It rarely happens. Still, a team monopolising the line-outs might prefer it to a scrum on the 22.

The throw-in: a round-up

Gain in ground. The throw-in happens at the place where the ball went directly into touch from any kick made inside the 22 (except a free kick awarded outside the 22) and from any penalty kick made anywhere. There can also be a gain in ground if the ball goes indirectly into touch – after first touching the ground or an opponent.

No gain in ground. Except for a penalty kick, if you're outside your 22 and you kick directly to touch, there is no gain in ground. This includes a free kick. If you take the ball into your 22 and kick directly to touch, there is no gain in ground. If you're awarded a free kick outside the 22 and you take that kick directly to touch from inside the 22, there is no gain in ground.

Quick throw-in

All it takes to throw the ball in from touch is the ball and someone to throw it. A line-out is an optional extra. If play moves so fast that most players are left far behind when the ball goes into touch, then the laws do more than allow a quick throw-in. They encourage it. Provided the line-out hasn't formed, the team with the right to throw in has the freedom to make a quick throw-in anywhere on the touch line between the place where the ball went out and their own goal line.

Think of that. Blues are playing Whites. The Blue full-back kicks from just inside his 22. He has dynamite in his boot. His kick finds touch deep in the White half. That's where the ball crosses the touch line, but where it lands is much further on. A White player catches it, runs to the touch line and takes a quick throw-in at a place only a couple of metres from his goal line. His full-back catches it and – with the aid of a following gale – hoofs it deep into the enemy half. Or he runs with it, jinks and swerves and side-steps through the entire opposition and scores the winning try. Listen, anything's possible. The point is, the White team used the freedom the laws gave them, and didn't wait for a line-out. Indeed, the player taking the quick throw-in need not wait for a team-mate. He can throw the ball in 5 metres, nip in-field and snap it up himself.

What's interesting here is the way the laws define the stretch of

Quick throw-in: how it's done. Play can re-start without a line-out. You can take a quick throw-in provided you use the same ball that went out and nobody else has touched it. You must throw it in straight, and at least five metres. A team-mate to catch it is an optional extra. You can run in-field and play the ball yourself.

5 METRES

touch line that's available for a quick throw-in: it's anywhere between the player's own goal line and the place where the ball went into touch. Now, that place may be a long way from where the ball would have been thrown in at a line-out. Take the example I just invented, Blues against Whites. Suppose the Blue full-back kicked from *outside* his 22. And suppose his kick went directly into touch. No gain in ground: the line-out would be opposite where he kicked. But if Whites attempt a quick throw-in, the furthest point upfield they can do it is where the ball went into touch. Worth remembering.

The freedom to take a quick throw-in is lightly hedged around with restrictions. You must use the same ball that went into touch. Nobody else must have touched the ball; that includes spectators. Notice that word 'touched'. If a team-mate even side-foots the ball to the thrower-in, that kills any chance of a quick throw-in. (If either of these things happens, any attempt at a quick throw-in is

Quick throw-in: where it's done. You can take a quick throw-in without waiting for a line-out to form. This quick throw-in can be taken anywhere on the touch line between the point where the ball went into touch and your own goal line. You must use the same ball that went out, and only you must have touched it.

disallowed – yet oddly enough the same team gets the throw-in at the subsequent line-out.)

A quick throw-in has to be straight, and it has to go five metres before the ball is played. If not, the opposing team gets the choice of *either* a line-out *or* a scrum on the 15-metre line – and note this: that line-out or scrum will not be where the regular line-out would have happened; it will be where the quick throw-in went wrong. You don't need much imagination to realise that this point could be a very long way from where the line-out would normally have been held. So it pays not to be sloppy when you take a quick throw-in.

One last thing. The line-out job description which you will read in the next chapter – all about the position of the furthest player, and the maximum distance of fifteen metres from touch, and so on – none of that applies to a quick throw-in. If you want to take a quick throw-in and you see a friendly face waiting twenty or thirty metres infield, chuck him a straight ball and the law will smile upon you both.

Readers write

C.M. of Hammersmith writes: Can you take a quick throw-in after an opponent's been tackled into touch? He held the ball in touch, so if you take it, it's been handled twice, hasn't it?

D.R. Technically, yes. But this is an exception. When an opponent's tackled into touch, if you grab the ball and take a quick throw-in, that's legal.

* * *

B.M. of Llanelli writes: A free kick's not much use if you can't score from it, is it? You can't even kick it direct to touch outside your 22 and gain ground. When I was a boy, a free kick was worth having.

D.R. It still gives you a bit of breathing space. It also creates a 10-metre gap between the teams. That's something. And if you're awarded a free kick just outside your 22, and you tap-kick and pass the ball into the 22, a team-mate can kick direct to touch and gain ground.

* * *

E.H. of Manhattan writes: I used to know a chap who could run down the touch line, with one foot in play and one foot out, dribbling the ball and always keeping it in the field-of-play.

D.R. Not easy, but legal.

* * *

A.K.K. of Chicago writes: If a team takes a quick throw-in, but they use the wrong ball or if it's been handled twice, the referee orders a line-out and he gives the throw-in to the same team. That's generous, isn't it?

D.R. Some might think so. Don't blame the referee; he's only doing what the law says. The thinking behind that law is this: play has not re-started, because the wrong ball was used. Therefore no offence took place, and so the same team keeps the throw-in. It's like an attempted drop-out taken from the wrong place. The game has not re-started, so the drop-out is taken again.

* * *

T.F.W. of Wellington writes: If there's a tree overhanging the field-of-play, and the ball hits a branch, is it in touch?

D.R. That's for the captains and the referee to decide, preferably before the kick-off.

* * *

A.C. of Liverpool writes: If two players (opponents) are holding the ball as they go into touch, who gets the throw-in?

D.R. The attacking team. That's the team in their opponents' half. Same applies when the referee can't decide who took or put the ball into touch.

* * *

R.H. of Exeter writes: If the ball goes into touch and bounces off a tree, can a player take a quick throw-in?

D.R. Yes. Same applies if the ball bounces off the clubhouse, or off an advertising board.

11
The line-out

The line-out is simply a way of getting the ball back into play, quickly and fairly, by throwing it along the line-of-touch. This line must be at least one metre from the goal line, so as to make room for the line-out. Play can restart without a line-out: *See Quick throw-in*. You can't take a quick throw-in once the line-out has formed, and there are certain guidelines about a formed line-out.

Usually, and especially towards the end of the second half, when the knees are buckling and hot flashes streak across the eyeballs, your average line-out begins to look like a bus queue in a typhoon.

All the faults which the players have been trying to avoid suddenly take over.

The line-out *should* be formed opposite the place where the touch-judge is signalling – but the players shamble up to a nearby spot and hope that the touch-judge will move over to them. The front of the line-out *should* be at least five metres from the touch-line – it's not; it's four, or three. The two lines *should* be straight and parallel to the goal-lines – but one line is pure switchback, and the other points right at the corner flag. There *should* be a clear space one metre wide down the middle – but it's clogged with bodies.

This is not the ideal way to restart the game.

The ideal line-out is a very simple thing. It is two straight lines, with a clear space of one metre (a yard and a bit) between them, one line per team and at least two players per line. The front of the line-out is at least five metres from touch, opposite the mark signalled by the touch-judge, and the back is no more than fifteen metres from touch.

Except after a penalty kick to touch, the man who throws the ball in is an opponent of the side which last touched the ball when it went out. It makes no difference if they didn't mean to touch it, or if

The line-out: before and after taking the medicine. Two views of a line-out – one all wrong, the other rather better. A line-out should have two single, straight, parallel lines, with a clear gap of one metre between the lines. The line-out should be at right angles to the place signalled by the touch judge. No player in the line-out should be less than five metres or more than fifteen metres from the touch line.

they were reluctantly forced into touch while holding the ball – they still lose it. Deciding which side throws the ball in is simply a matter of deciding who last touched it, and giving it to the other side. (The benefit of the doubt goes to the attacking team.)

The player throwing in – usually the hooker – must stand in touch and throw the ball so that it goes at least five metres at right angles to the touch-line before it touches a player or the ground.

Now, the laws say that he has to throw the ball *along the line-of-touch*, which is an imaginary line running through the touch-judge and across the field, parallel to the goal lines. (So it follows that the line-out forms up on either side of the line-of-touch.) The purpose of a line-out is to re-start play quickly *and fairly*. Both sides must be given a reasonable chance of getting the ball, and if there's a small gale blowing from left to right, it's obvious that a short, hard throw stands a better chance of landing in the right place than a long lob.

If the player throwing in makes a hash of it – stands in the wrong place, or doesn't throw it five metres, or doesn't throw it in straight – the other side can choose either to take the throw-in themselves or to have a scrum fifteen metres in. If they decide to have a second throw-in and they too get it wrong, then the referee orders a scrum.

As the hooker stands poised to lob the ball, picture the scene: two single, straight and parallel lines, starting five metres in and separated by a healthy respect for the invisible line-of-touch. Bear all that in mind while we have a bash at the next bit, which affects so much of the line-out that we might as well do it now: the dreaded (but really simple) *line-out offside*.

Line-out offside

'People,' Marx* once observed, 'come in two sorts. There's the workers, who do the grafting; and there's the rest, who get the benefit.'

He was talking, of course, about the line-out, which is divided for the purposes of offside into:

1 those taking part
2 those not taking part.

* Dr Henry Marx, perhaps the heaviest-ever forward to play for Rutland.

Those taking part are all the players involved in throwing the ball in, catching it, and disposing of it. In chronological order they are the man with the ball (and his opposite number), all the forwards standing in the line-out, and the one player of each team in position to receive the ball from the line-out – usually (but not necessarily) the scrum-halves.

Those not taking part are all the others – the backs (stand-offs, centres, wings, full-backs) and any forwards who have chosen not to join the line-out.

Where the backs can stand. The offside line for players not taking part in the line-out (usually, but not exclusively, the backs) lies ten metres behind the line-out – or it is the goal line, if that's nearer. Until the line-out ends, all players not in it must stay behind that line. The only exceptions are the scrum-half, who can stand between the two, and one opponent (usually the hooker) of the player throwing in the ball. This opponent can be in the 5-metre area.

A serious case of impetuosity. Until the ball is thrown in, the line-out offside line runs down the middle. Once it's thrown in, it runs through the ball. Either way, the nearest White player has gone too far. In his desire to cream the stand-off he has got himself thoroughly offside.

Offside for those taking part in the line-out

Until the ball is thrown in, the offside line for those taking part is the line-of-touch. No player must put a foot across this imaginary line, unless he's jumping for the ball; and if he jumps and misses he must hustle back without delay.

As soon as the ball is thrown in and it has touched a player or the ground, the offside line runs through the ball itself. Every player in the line-out must stay on his own side of the ball until the line-out is over. (And if you don't know when that is, don't worry, we'll get to it later.)

So offside for players taking part in a line-out is quite straight-forward. Until the ball is thrown in, keep behind the line-of-touch; after that, keep behind the ball.

Offside for those not taking part in the line-out

The offside line for players *not* taking part is even simpler. It's a line ten metres behind the line-of-touch (which is like saying ten metres behind the line-out) and parallel to the goal lines, or the goal-line itself, if that happens to be nearer. And as before, all players *not* taking part in the line-out must keep both feet behind their offside line until the line-out is over. (In the case of the goal line they can keep both feet *on* the line, since the line is in the in-goal.)

If you have this situation clearly imprinted on what for want of a better word we may call the mind, you will see that it creates an area up to twenty metres wide between the opposing back-lines. Whichever side wins the ball from the line-out is rewarded with a healthy acreage of sod in which to start hatching its devilish plots before the foe can pour across no-man's-land and start making nuisances of themselves.

This is what the law is for. There is no point in winning the ball if you get a tackle like a Turkish earthquake immediately after it. Once the line-out is over the forwards can set off and do their worst, but it has been proved repeatedly that the ball can travel faster than the man. (Ask any forward.) What's more, the forwards are limited by the *length* (in distance) of the line-out.

The length of the line-out

The line-out begins five metres from touch and ends fifteen metres from touch. No line-out player is allowed to stand more than fifteen metres from touch. This means that the actual line of players can never be more than ten metres long.

However, the side throwing in has some influence on the length of the line-out, because it has the privilege of deciding how many players may take part in the line-out. If it chooses to have fewer than usual, its opponents cannot exceed that number. Suppose the team throwing in opts for a three-man line-out. The other team must not have more than three men in that line-out. But those three are not obliged to stand opposite their opponents; they can place themselves wherever they wish, right up to the fifteen-metre mark.

But not beyond it. Occasionally a flanker will absentmindedly wander a yard or so beyond the mark. If the referee doesn't notice this, you can be sure the opposing half-backs will. If they get the ball, that yard or so will give the flanker an unfair start when he pressures the No. 10. Back-markers who drift infield before the line-out has ended are offside. They should be penalised.

When the line-out begins

The instant the ball leaves the hands of the player throwing it in, the line-out has begun and large gentlemen with hands like dinnerplates can start launching themselves upwards. And until the line-out ends, all line-out players must stay inside the fifteen-metre mark. (There is one exception to this: a *long throw-in* over the tail of the line-out; but that's not really a line-out at all. We get to long throw-ins a bit later.)

Even when the ball has left the hands of the player throwing it in, that doesn't give the line-out men a free hand. They must keep that metre-wide space between the lines unless they're actually jumping for the ball, until the ball has touched a player or the ground. This strikes me as a pretty broad exception, because everyone in the line-out *can* jump for the ball, if they want to. But according to law, that one-metre gap should survive until the ball has touched someone or something.

When the line-out ends

The line-out ends when one of four things happens:

1 The ball leaves the line-out.
2 A player with the ball leaves the line-out.
3 The ball is thrown beyond the last man in the line-out.
4 A ruck or maul has formed, and the *whole* of the ruck or maul moves beyond the line-of-touch.

When any one of those things has happened, the line-out is over and line-out offside is a thing of the past. In the case of the first three, the ball is in open play and anyone can go anywhere. In the case of the fourth – where a ruck or maul has formed – the offside law for rucks or mauls applies (obviously). So the back-lines can immediately move up to the tail-ends of the ruck or maul.

Notice that the line-out comes to an end, not when a ruck or maul forms, but when that ruck or maul has completely moved away from the line-of-touch (that's the imaginary line running through the middle of the line-out). A ruck or maul in a line-out is still a line-out, and so the back-lines must stay ten metres behind it. What's more, any line-out player who does not join the ruck or maul must retire to its offside line, which runs through its tail-end, and stay there.

Thus a line-out that develops into a ruck or maul presents the line-out players with three separate and distinct offside lines in quick succession. The first line, before the ball has been thrown in, is the line-of-touch. The second line, after the ball has been thrown in and touched something or someone, runs through the ball itself. If a ruck or maul forms the third line runs through the tail of the ruck or maul. All three can happen in the space of a few seconds, so line-out players need to keep their wits about them.

When the ruck or maul gives a convulsive shudder and lurches clear of the line-out – all of it, not just most of it – then the line-out has ended and the ruck/maul is promoted to Grade A status, with its own offside lines, luncheon vouchers, pension schemes, and so on.

And *that* is the moment when the back-line can, without fear of savage reprisals, nip smartly forward. It pays to know just when you can make that move without risking a penalty kick between your uprights. That's why I'm telling you all this.

Incidentally, the referee can end a line-out if he decides the ball has become unplayable. The game restarts with a scrum.

Where the ball-thrower can go. Also the scrum-half

While all this crucial decision-making is going on, what of the man who threw the ball in? He has done his bit – thrown it to number three in the line-out, Big Bert, only Bert wasn't quite ready so the other side caught it – and now he's watching rather anxiously, wondering what he can do to help.

After he has thrown in the ball there are only four things which the thrower (and his opposite number) can do, legally, until the line-out's over:

1 Stay where he is, between the line-out and the touch-line.
2 Get stuck into the line-out.
3 Nip round the side and play scrum-half, provided nobody else is doing it.
4 Get ten metres back.

If either of the scrum-halves sees a gap in the line-out, he can flit into it and take the ball, just as long as he doesn't go barging into or obstructing an opponent.

Once the ball's been thrown in, what most hookers do is lurk in the space between touch and the front of the line-out. That's fine, as long as they stay behind the ball. Occasionally, however, a hooker wanders forward, just a couple of paces but it's enough. Enough to what? Display his presence and thereby persuade the opposing scrum-half to forget about attacking down the touch-line. So bang goes one option. The hooker's offside, he's influencing play, he ought to be penalised. So should flankers who sometimes work a similar racket at the back of the line-out, taking a little walk across the offside line in order to discourage the scrum-half from attacking around the tail. Bang goes another option. Scandalous.

Peeling-off

The law book, you will recall, goes to some lengths to spell out who is in the line-out and who is not. And it goes to considerable lengths – ten metres – to separate the two. Naturally, having done this, it wants to keep up the good work until the line-out is over. If you are ten metres back, you must not wander forward. If you are in the line-out, you must not stray back. Only one man can stand between the line-out and the back-line, and he is the scrum-half.

On the other hand, once the ball has been thrown in you can't expect the forwards to stand on one leg while they watch who catches it. They want to do their little bit to help, and that often means unplugging themselves from the line at spot A in order to get stuck in again at Spot B. That, as the actress said to the bishop, is only human nature.

The laws, in their boundless wisdom, allow this. At the same

Peeling-off – yes. Two scrum-halves – no. Any line-out player can peel off as soon as the ball leaves the hands of the player throwing in, provided the peeler moves close to and parallel to the line-out. He can catch the ball if it's knocked or passed back. What he must not do is take up a position as an extra scrum-half. The law allows only one scrum-half per team at a line-out. Penalty: Free kick.

time, they keep a tight grip on players who are peeling-off.

For a start, you must not begin to peel off until the ball has left the thrower's hands. Then, you must keep close to the line of the line-out. Otherwise, the penalty is a free kick on the 15-metre line.

How close is 'close'? How high is the sky? Look at it this way: at a line-out the scrum-half is a privileged player, because he's allowed to stand between the line-out and his back-line. Each team is allotted one scrum-half, and you can't increase that number by having spare forwards falling back from the line. If the referee sees a forward standing alongside the scrum-half, he's more likely to think that he's doubling up than that he's peeling off.

How close is 'close'? Nobody knows. But a good rule-of-thumb whenever you're peeling off is to be where you can reach out and touch the line-out. Anywhere deeper than that is a bit dodgy, especially if you're taking a pass or knock-back.

Line-out offside round-up

Here, then, is a quick wrap-up of the various ways you can be offside at a line out.

Offside at the front of the line-out. The line-out begins five metres from touch. If you stand nearer to touch than that, you are offside (except the relevant throwers-in). However, once the ball has been thrown beyond you, you can move into that space at the front.

Stepping out of line. Each line of forwards must leave a clear space one metre wide down the middle until the ball is thrown in. If you move into this space before the ball is thrown in, you're offside.

Overstepping the ball. Once the ball has been thrown in, the offside line runs through the ball. If you get in front of it, you're offside. However, if you got there because you were genuinely jumping for the ball, you'll be given a chance to get back onside.

Offside at the back of the line-out. Until the line-out ends, the furthest player in a line-out must not be more than fifteen metres from touch, or he will be offside.

Peeling-off too soon or too deep. If you peel off before the ball has been thrown in, or if you peel off and move or stand too far from the line-out, you are offside.

Not ten metres back. If you're not taking part in the line-out you must stay ten metres behind it. If you don't get back far enough, or if you advance too soon, you're offside.

I fancy I hear ugly mutterings from the back of the hall. Evidently there are those who feel that rugby, far from being the simple sport I promised, has developed into something bloody diabolical, so can they have their money back?

Stick with it, lads. Rugby *is* a simple game, even including line-out offside.

The thing about the line-out is that whilst there are no end of complicated ways of getting *offside*, there is only one, very simple way to stay *onside*. Master that, and you're home and dry.

The line-out has a simple shape. It starts here and it stops there, and between these ends are two straight, single lines. Stay in line until the ball arrives, and keep behind the ball until the line-out ends and you won't go far wrong.

You can always find trouble if you go looking for it; but in that case don't blame the laws for making life difficult. It's really your option.

Keeping what's left of your nose clean

There are a couple of other things which the laws would rather you didn't do in a line-out. Most of them can be summed up in these two commandments:

1 Until the ball is thrown in, don't touch anyone.
2 After the ball is thrown in, don't touch an opponent unless he has the ball, or unless a ruck or maul has formed.

Don't barge

If there is a clear space down the middle you shouldn't be touching an opponent. Most barging takes place when players are jumping for the ball and one player is more concerned with putting his shoulder into his opponent than getting his hands on the ball. This is illegal, and can even be dangerous: a player jumping at full stretch is very vulnerable to a bash in the ribs. (Even a sly nudge can unbalance him.) Line-out bargers are bad news. Good refs nobble them fast.

Don't obstruct

You've seen it; I've seen it; we've all seen it, and not a few of us have done it. The ball is thrown in, it bounces about, someone taps it back and it lands on the deck. The scrum-half goes after it, the opposing forwards *try* to go after it, and a wall of arms holds them back. This is obstruction. You must not hold or push or deliberately obstruct an opponent who hasn't got the ball. The urge to protect your winnings is strong. It is tempting to fling out an arm and hold your opponent back, and it is easy, and it is illegal.

This is true of all parts of the game, of course. It's just that obstruction seems more natural in a line-out. Players who wouldn't think of grabbing an opponent to keep him from tackling someone in open play will feel that they are being quite noble by holding off an opponent who has designs on their scrum-half.

There is, I suppose, a bit of a difference. A line-out by its very nature presents a wall of brawn between one lot of forwards and their opponents' scrum-half, and the brawn has every right to

Protecting the winnings – but it's obstruction. In any part of the game it is illegal to obstruct an opponent who hasn't got the ball – and that goes for line-outs too.

arrange itself in such a way that nobody can get through. But what it hasn't got a right to do is to grab, barge, or deliberately obstruct any opponent who would otherwise have got through. You're entitled to *be* in his way but not to *get* in his way.

Don't use your outside arm only

You must not use your outside arm alone to catch or deflect the ball. Use both of your arms, or just the inner arm. (If both hands are above your head you can use either hand to play the ball.) Why? Read on.

Don't lever yourself up on an opponent

When this happens, the arm that the line-out player uses in order to lever himself up (and his opponent down) is the inside arm, because it is nearer his opponent's shoulder. Now you know why outer-arm catching is illegal. The laws reckon that, if the inner arm isn't reaching up for the ball, who knows what dirty work it might get up to?

Don't jump or support before the ball is thrown

You must not jump before the ball has left the hands of the thrower-in. Similarly, you must not support the jumper until the ball is on its way. Once the ball is thrown, he can jump and you can help him. Not before.

Don't ankle-tap the jumper

If, as your opponents' ace jumper launches himself into space, it occurs to you to stay down at ground level, wait for his feet to come up to you, and then remove them, you're both in trouble. He may be badly injured and you will certainly be heavily penalised. Tackling or pulling the feet of a jumper while he's in the air is dangerous play.

Support versus levering. Any line-out player jumping for the ball must get off the deck by his own efforts. Once he's airborne, a team-mate can help him stay up. That's legal. But if a player levers himself up on an opponent, that's a penalty kick. Levering means playing the man without the ball, which is foul play. What's more, the levering jumper is using only his outside arm to win the ball. That too is illegal.

Don't block the throw-in

The throw-in must travel at least five metres from touch, which is why a line-out player must not be less than five metres from touch. Not surprisingly, if he stands less than five metres, and if he blocks the throw-in, he'll get penalised.

The too-short throw-in

The short throw-in to the front man in the line-out is a thing you see fairly often, and if players knew how risky it was they would turn grey. Pseudo-scientific research has shown that as often as nine times out of ten, the ball doesn't travel the minimum of five metres.

When this is the result of tired blood on the part of the gent throwing it in, the referee may give him a pitying glance and let the other team have a go. But when the problem is the greed and impetuosity of a front marker in the line-out who can't wait for the ball to come to him and who invades the five-metre strip in order to get it first, that's different. That's a free kick to his opponents.

Blocking the throw. At a line-out the throw-in must travel at least five metres, and nobody must stop this. Here a line-out player is standing less than five metres from the touch line and blocking the throw-in, so he's in trouble two ways. Penalty: Free kick.

Rare and unusual line-outs

Not every line-out has all the stirring pageantry and solemn ritual described above. Some are short, scarcely as long as they are wide. Some are full-length, yet they never receive the ball because it goes clean over them. Both kinds are perfectly legal.

Short line-out

The minimum number of players in a line-out is two from each side, and if the side throwing the ball in decides that a two-man line is a good idea, their opponents have no choice but to go along with them.

If, however, the side throwing in already *has* seven men in the line-out, they cannot decide then to pull five of them out and leave two; it's too late for that. The decision must be made *before* these players formed up in the line-out. Once they're in they must stay there until the line-out's over.

Opponents of the side throwing the ball in are given a bit of leeway, though. Since they don't know how many men the other side is going to put into its line, they've got to prepare for the worst. Then, if it turns out to be a short line, the referee will give them a reasonable amount of time to withdraw the extra players before the ball is thrown in.

For instance, if Blues kick the ball into touch a yard from Whites' goal-line, and get ready for an orthodox, seven-man line-out, Whites might decide to form a short, two-man line and hold the other five in readiness in their in-goal. In that case, Blues would be given time to pull out five of *their* forwards, before Whites go ahead and throw the ball in.

Long throw-in

The invisible line-of-touch stretches – in theory – right across the field, and if you've got a man who can throw it that far there's nothing to stop him hurling the ball right past the line-out and into the wide open spaces – as long as it pitches on the line-of-touch.

As soon as the ball leaves his hands, any player in the line-out or out of it – forward, scrum-half or back – can run out to catch this long throw-in. The backs can run forward, and the forwards or scrum-half can run beyond the 15-metre mark. But if they anticipate a long throw-in which doesn't then take place – if the ball is not in fact thrown to them or beyond them – they're offside.

Throwing in straight is the crucial part of the line-out. Any discussion of long throw-ins is so much wasted breath when the player throwing the ball in has an effective range of about fifteen metres, and that only on days of flat calm. Show me a long throw-in where the ball has travelled more than twenty metres, and I'll show you a seven-to-four chance that it didn't go straight. Seven-to-four? Make it eight-to-three.

Penalties for line-out offences

As with scrums, so with line-outs. Faults and follies are penalised *either* by a free kick *or* by a penalty kick. Free-kick offences are mostly technical errors, whereas penalty kicks get handed out for serious crimes.

For example, a free kick is given for 'spacing' offences – where a player fails to leave a metre-wide gap between the lines, or he stands less than five metres or more than fifteen metres from touch when the line-out forms; for delaying or dummying the throw-in; for a 'numbers' offence – having too many players in the line; for levering on a team-mate's shoulder; for hoisting a team-mate; for using only the outside arm to catch the ball; or for peeling-off too soon or too deep.

By contrast, it's a penalty kick if you barge an opponent, or lever yourself up by using him as a support; or if you get yourself offside in any of the various ways I've already described; or if you hold or shoulder or obstruct an opponent who hasn't got the ball.

Touch judges

There are two of these officials, one for each touch-line, and their job is to help the referee by following play up and down and signalling (with a small flag provided for the purpose) whenever the ball goes into touch, or touch-in-goal. In the case of a high kick, this may involve some fast geometrical calculation between the ears: what matters is where the ball crosses the line, not where it comes to earth.

The touch-judge also signals which side is entitled to throw the ball in, so he has to decide who last touched the ball. If the kick was made outside the kicker's 22, the touch-judge has to decide whether or not it went directly into touch, and locate the throw-in accordingly – although the referee can over-rule him. It's for the referee to decide whether or not a player was outside his 22, and exactly where the throw-in should take place.

It's important that the touch-judge should flourish his flag the very moment the ball goes into touch. Often the referee is watching for this signal because, what with all the dust and steam, he can't actually see the ball.

Once the referee has whistled for touch, the touch-judge should stand at the appropriate spot, still keeping his flag up so that everyone can see him, and point to whichever side is to throw the ball in. Having done this, he should keep on doing it and above all *stay where he is* until the ball has been thrown in. If the players line up in the wrong place, the touch-judge should hold his ground, perhaps flaring the nostrils a little. What he should not do is feebly shuffle sideways. Just because they've got it wrong, there's no need for him to get it wrong, too.

If the wrong team throws the ball in, or if the man who throws it in steps in the field-of-play, or if a replacement ball or a twice-handled ball is used at a quick throw-in, the touch judge should keep his flag up as a signal to the referee – who can always overrule him and let play go on.

The touch-judges also help the referee when kicks at goal are being taken – penalty kicks or conversions. (For penalty kicks, where the kicker can decide whether or not to go for goal, the referee usually signals the touch-judges to come round behind the posts, using a sweeping gesture rather like a druid loosening up before a big sunrise.) One touch-judge stands at or behind each goal post; if the ball goes over the bar he raises his flag.

If the ball goes directly over the top of the post he doesn't raise his flag. The posts are considered to soar heavenwards indefinitely. If the ball went over one it must have hit it.

You might think that this is a lot of needless fuss about a rather dreary part of the game, and you would be completely wrong. Anyone who has played in a game where one touch-judge was eleven and always gave the ball to the home team because his big brother was playing on that wing, and the other touch-judge was eighty-three and never got closer than forty yards to the action all afternoon, knows that good touch-judging is worth having.

It's the responsibility of the team captains to produce touch-judges, and the traditional arrangement is for the teams to provide one each. Or so it should be. In a great many clubs, the tradition is to forget all about it until the referee asks, and then shout vaguely in the direction of the crowd of drinkers outside the clubhouse. The results are usually disastrous, but that doesn't stop the players complaining bitterly about unfair or inaccurate decisions. But then, nothing will.

Many people don't realise that the touch-judges come under the control of the referee just as the players do. If a touch-judge turns out to be clueless or crooked, the referee can ask for him to be replaced; and if the touch-judge goes completely bananas the referee can order him off the playing enclosure and report him to the Union for misconduct. It's not just an academic point. I've come across touch-judges who became quite crazed and began beating visiting players over the head with their flags. I even knew one touch-judge who, while his team were preparing to take a kick at goal, used to toss up little handfuls of grass to help the kicker gauge the wind-strength. He was quite surprised when the referee (me) told him to stop.

Most touch-judges aren't like that. The higher up the game you go the better they are, until at top matches the touch-judges will be highly qualified referees who are good enough to take over the whistle if the appointed referee gets injured. In these matches the touch-judges have been given extra powers: if they see dangerous play or misconduct they must signal the fact to the referee. The touch-judge does this by raising his flag to the horizontal and pointing it infield. That signal does not stop the game; but at the next stoppage the referee goes over to the touch-judge, finds out what happened, and takes action accordingly.

Readers write

P.B. of Perth, WA writes: Remember that stuff about blokes who peel off having to stay close to the line-out? That's guff. They never do, and they never get penalised.

D.R. I hear what you say.

*   *   *

H.G. of Vancouver writes: Every line-out I ever see, the two separate lines vanish the instant the ball gets thrown in. They all just merge into a mob.

D.R. I hear you, too.

*   *   *

T.T. of Gloucester writes: I agree that a line-out jumper must not use his outside arm alone to get the ball, but there's an exception you didn't mention.

D.R. Yes? What's that?

T.T. We've got a one-armed lock forward. Half the time, when he's jumping, he has no inside arm.

D.R. Astonishing.

*   *   *

P.J. O'H. of Garryowen writes: If it's blowing a gale, you've no choice but to throw-in crooked, or it won't come down straight.

D.R. A man's gotta do what a man's gotta do.

*   *   *

L.R.N. of Johannesburg writes: What's so terrible about jumping and lifting before the throw-in? Get the jumper up in the air, where the thrower can see the guy!

D.R. I've got a better idea. Let's all build human pyramids, and forget the rugby.

* * *

B.D. of Orrell writes: I've calculated that, at any line-out, a maximum of ninety-three separate offences can take place.

D.R. You missed a couple.

* * *

J.Y. of Tokyo writes: Up until 1946, you could choose to take a scrum instead of a line-out.

D.R. Stick around. Who knows? That day may return.

* * *

S.G. of Wolverhampton writes: What's all this I keep on hearing about the Team of Three?

D.R. It's not in the laws, but it's worth knowing about. The three are the referee and his touch judges, and at the top level of games – where touch judges are very competent – they work as a team.

S.G. Doing what?

D.R. The touch judge can signal Dangerous Play or Misconduct, of course, but he can spot lesser offences too – for instance at the line-out – and keep the referee informed. He also helps by indicating when a quick throw-in is allowable or not. The Team of Three gives the referee two extra pairs of eyes.

12
Scoring

The aim of the game is to score points. The best way to do this is by scoring tries.

Naturally, any team should have at least one man who can kick penalty goals from all parts of the field-of-play and adjoining counties. Nevertheless, a try can bring you a maximum of seven points. Any other score is worth only three. The moral is obvious.

Try

You score a try by being the first to ground the ball in your opponents' in-goal, and this is worth five points. You don't have to carry the ball across the line: you can chase someone else's kick or pass, and fall on it, or you can kick it ahead yourself and follow up and score. In fact the only thing you must be sure of is *grounding the ball* – which is not necessarily the same as touching it down, or touching it when it's on the ground. For instance, picking up the ball in the in-goal is not grounding it (so you can pick it up and run towards the posts if you want to improve the chances of conversion).

Grounding the ball

You can ground the ball in one of three ways. If you are holding it you can simply touch it to the ground. Some people think that it's necessary to press down, but it's not. They are thinking of the second method: if the ball is already on the ground, you must press down on it with your hands or arms (one is enough). Alternatively, if the ball is already on the ground you can fall on it so that it's under

The meaning of grounding. You score a try by grounding the ball in the in-goal. There are three ways of grounding the ball: (a) hold it and touch the ground with it; (b) press down on it when it's on the ground; (c) fall on it so that it's under your front anywhere between waist and neck.

the front of your body anywhere from the waist to the neck. Note that in this way you don't have to lay a finger on the ball. You can ground a ball, and score a try, simply by diving on top of it and hitting it with your shoulder, chest or stomach – provided you get there first.

On the other hand, if you *are* holding the ball, make quite sure that the referee has seen you touch it down. Occasionally you will see a player race fifty yards, swerving out of seven or eight tackles, beat the full-back with almost contemptuous ease, stroll over the line between the posts, and deposit the ball without so much as breaking stride. The sad thing is that he hasn't actually *touched the ball down*: he got within an inch or two of the turf and then gracefully let go, like a goose demonstrating the laying of a golden egg. And if the referee was paying close attention, then he won't have blown for a try.

It pays to let everyone see that you have actually grounded the ball; and any player who is so pleased with his brilliant approach work that he neglects this finishing touch is asking for trouble. It's not that the referee is being bloody-minded, it's just that he has no alternative. He can't say to himself, 'Stone me, that feller deserves a try after a run like that, even though he didn't really score one,' can he? He must do what the laws say.

Personally, if I had galloped fifty yards with the ball – well, let's be realistic: if I had lumbered ten yard with the ball and gone over the goal line, I would slam it down good and hard. And if I didn't hear the whistle I'd keep leaning on the ball until either the referee blew or I woke up and realized I'd only crossed the enemy 22.

Some players believe that an attacker who drops the ball when he has crossed the goal line cannot score a try. They are wrong. Dropping the ball is not an offence unless it's thrown or knocked forward. If it falls straight down, and the attacker then grounds it, that's a try. Why not?

Not seen. If you were the referee, would you give a try here? Bear in mind that a basic principle of refereeing is: Never guess. If you didn't see it, you can't give it. Sometimes even the best of referees can't see the ball because so many players are in the way. A try is not a try unless the referee can see it being scored.

Where are the lines?

The goal line is part of the in-goal, so you can score a try by grounding the ball on the goal line. The goal posts are also part of the in-goal, and if you have grounded the ball so that it is touching your opponents' goal post, you've scored. Whether or not the referee will agree with you is another matter, and there is no doubt that it's safer to get the ball right inside the in-goal.

The touch-in-goal lines and the dead-ball line are not in the in-goal, so you can't score on them. The corner flag, since we're picking so many nits, is part of touch-in-goal, but the flag – the actual cloth – is not; it's nowhere; it doesn't exist, in law.

Pushover try

A scrum can score a try. If one team shoves so hard that they push their opponents back over their goal-line and then ground the ball, it's a try. The cardinal sin of handling in the scrum doesn't apply, for the glaringly obvious reason that there is no scrum once it has

Tackled and reaching out to score. If you get tackled so near to your opponents' goal line that you can immediately reach out and ground the ball on or over the line, that's a try. This is true even if the ball has already touched the ground.

Momentum try. If you get tackled short of your opponents' goal line, but your momentum is so great that it takes you into the in-goal and you ground the ball, that's a try. If you crawl to the goal line, it's not.

crossed the goal line; a scrum can take place only in the field-of-play, and if the ball in the scrum touches or crosses the goal line the scrum has ended. If the *defenders* take the ball into their in-goal during a pushover and they ground it, this is considered a touch-down and leads to a five-metre scrum.

Sliding over to score

If you get tackled when you're hurtling for the line, but your hurtle is so momentous that it carries you over and you ground the ball, that is a try, even if the ball has already touched the field-of-play on the way. It's all a question of momentum. Your thrust has to be so irresistible that it carries you into the in-goal.

Reaching out to score

You can even reach out and score, even when you've been tackled short of the line and brought to a full stop. I should warn you that there are strong differences of opinion about this. The problem is combining parts of two separate laws.

The law about tries says that a tackled player scores a try if he's tackled in such a position that he 'is able to place the ball on or over the goal line' – and here comes the tricky bit – 'whilst complying with the Law'. Which law? It can only be the tackle law. And the tackle law says that, although a tackled player must release the ball, he is allowed 'to put the ball on the ground in any direction', provided he does so immediately.

Combine those two items, and you get a situation where the player is tackled just short of the line. We know the tackle law lets him 'put the ball on the ground in any direction'. Common sense says this means he can reach out and put it down, otherwise why say 'in any direction'? So, if the goal line is within his reach, he can score – provided he acts immediately.

What the tackled player must not do is try to crawl or squirm or struggle to the line. That is not immediate action. Reaching out is done with the arm or arms, not the body.

Scoring from touch

If the ball is in the enemy's in-goal and you are in touch or touch-in-goal, you can fall on it and score. If you pick it up, of course, you're an idiot.

Penalty try

If a defender does something unfair or illegal which, in the referee's opinion, prevents a *probable* try, then he will award a penalty try. If he thinks the foul play probably prevented a try being scored in a better place, he'll award a penalty try. The interesting word here is 'probably'. The referee doesn't have to be absolutely convinced that a try would inevitably have been scored; he just has to feel sure that the attacking side had a healthy odds-on chance. With that in mind, he can award a penalty try for an offence in mid-field just as much as for one inside the defenders' 22. A penalty try is always given between the posts. Contrary to an ancient myth, the defenders *can* charge the kick at goal.

Converting a try

Scoring a try gives a team the right to attempt to convert it into a goal (that's why it's called a 'try') by taking a kick at goal. A conversion is worth a further two points. The kick is taken exactly in front of the spot where the try was scored: anywhere on a line through the place of score, parallel with the touch-line. If the try was scored between the posts, it's a short, easy kick from right in front. If the try was scored in the corner, it's a long, hard kick from near touch. The kick can be a place-kick or a drop-kick. (But see Seven-a-Side Variations at the end of this book.) Anyone on the scoring side may take the kick, and he can have a placer to hold the ball if he wants. All the rest of his team must get behind the ball, and all their opponents must be behind the goal line until the kicker begins his run-up or offers to kick. They can then charge or jump and try to deflect the ball, but even if they touch it and it goes over the bar, the goal is good.

Conversion kick. This is taken opposite the place where the try was scored. Defenders must stay behind their goal line until the kicker starts his run-up. Then they can charge, wave or jump – but not shout. Contrary to myth, you can charge the conversion kick after a penalty try.

What they must not do is shout as they charge. If they do, or if they offend in any other way – charge too soon, for instance – the referee can allow the same kicker to take a second kick without any charge. If, despite the defenders' wrongdoing, the first kick goes over, then the referee lets it stand and chalks up two points to the forces of righteousness.

Should any of the kicker's team be crazy enough to be in front of the ball when kicked, the kick doesn't count. (Until recently, the same was true if a team-mate held the ball and the ball didn't touch the ground before it got kicked out of the placer's hands. The ball wasn't grounded, so it wasn't considered a proper kick. Nowadays, with plastic kicking tees, the ball is never grounded; so that little bit of law has been quietly dropped.)

It's not uncommon for the ball to fall over before the kicker has started his run. If it does, the referee should give him permission to tee it up again. If it falls over *after* he's started his run, he must carry on with his kick. This means that if it not only falls over but also rolls away, he may end up kicking it from a spot which is some little distance from the line through the place where the try was scored; nevertheless it's a goal if he gets the ball over the crossbar. On the other hand, if the ball falls over and rolls into touch, that's the end: no second kick allowed.

Get on with it

The laws make it clear that all kicks, including conversions, must be taken without delay. That means the kicker must not be 'unreasonably slow', and if you want to know how slow is unreasonable, it's whatever the referee thinks. Circumstances vary, and he might be more tolerant in a rainstorm than during a flat calm. The laws give him some guidance: they say that a period of one minute between the time the player indicates he's going to kick at goal and the moment he actually kicks it is not too long. You'd think a minute was ample time to tee the ball up and take a hopeful pot at goal. Usually it is. The trouble is that many teams are so stunned by success that they leave the ball lying and forget all about the kick. By the time they've got hold of a kicker, and he has got hold of the ball, the first minute has about eight seconds left. That, of course, is entirely their fault; and if the referee were to disallow the kick and proceed at once to the centre of the field, they might wake up next time. No team has a right to waste its opponents' time.

Indeed, even if the kicker takes a full minute to bring off a kick at goal, no more than forty seconds of playing time will be lost, because the referee will simply add on the extra kicking time at the end of that half of the match, just as he already adds on any injury time. This applies whether or not he considers that the kicker has taken unnecessarily long over his kick. A kick at goal can take more than forty seconds, but it can never use up more than forty seconds of playing time.

If you think that all this stopwatching is a bit superfluous, it isn't. There is a good reason for keeping a tight rein on these delays. Kicks at goal can easily total fifteen or even twenty minutes, which means up to one quarter of playing time. Check out a few games for yourself if you don't believe me.

It's not essential to waste any time at all after you've scored a try, of course. The conversion attempt is optional; you needn't take it if you don't want to. This has happened – usually right at the end of a game when the scoring side needed more than two points to win, and preferred to use the remaining time in an attempt to score another try. It has been known to succeed, too.

Penalty goal

Apart from tries and conversions, you can score points in two other ways: by a penalty goal or a dropped goal. Each is worth three points.

A penalty goal must be either a place kick or a drop kick in the field-of-play, and of course the ball has to go over the opponents' crossbar. (You can read all about penalty kicks in the chapter on Kicks.)

During a kick at goal, defenders must stand still, hands by their sides, from the start of the kicker's run until he kicks the ball. If they misbehave while the penalty kick is being taken but the ball goes over just the same, the referee will give a goal. If it doesn't go over, he can award a second kick ten metres further forward. And if he thinks that the ball would *probably* have gone over if a defender hadn't illegally got in its way, he can even award a goal without the ball crossing the bar at all.

The time limits for penalty kicks at goal are the same as those for conversion attempts: one minute is usually regarded as not excessive, and even so, everything over forty seconds is made up in the same half of the match.

Dropped goal

You can score a dropped goal (three points) any time the game is going on, except from a free kick or at a kick-off or drop-out. All you have to do is drop-kick the ball from the field-of-play over your opponents' cross-bar. Even if an opponent touches the ball (or *vice versa*) before it goes over, it is still a goal. This applies to all kicks at goal. But if you drop-kick for goal and the ball touches one of your *own* players before going over, it's no goal – not because he may have diverted it but because he must have been, at the very least, accidentally offside.

A dropped goal need not be the slick, well-oiled action you normally associate with international half-backs. All that is required is a drop kick that sneaks over the bar; and a drop kick is simply a ball that has been dropped and kicked after the first bounce. If you get tackled in the enemy 22, drop the ball in a blind panic, lash out and kick it on the first bounce, and accidentally send it flying between the posts, that's worth three points. Crummy points, but they all count.

Odds and Sods

Blown back; hitting the woodwork

If the ball goes over the cross-bar and the wind blows it back, a goal is scored. (This ruling was made in 1885, so blowing back probably happened for the first time in 1884. The winter of '84 was terribly windy, I remember.) If the ball hits a goal post, or both goal posts, or the cross-bar, or all three, and then goes over the bar, a goal is scored. If the ball goes directly over the top of a goal post it's not a goal; but you knew that already.

No goal from a free kick

And not just from a free kick. If a player tap-kicks a free kick and passes to a team-mate, *that* player cannot score a dropped goal, either. In fact, the team given a free kick can't score a dropped goal until after an opponent has played the ball, or after an opponent has made a tackle, or after a maul has formed, or after the ball is dead. So free kicks and dropped goals are just about incompatible.

Illegally deflected but still a goal

At all types of kick at goal – conversion, penalty goal or dropped goal – if the referee reckons that the ball would *probably* have gone over if a defender hadn't illegally touched it, he can award a goal even though the ball never reached its target. Hard to imagine a defender getting his hands on a penalty kick in full flight, but he might be able to do it to a conversion kick or a dropped kick. Suppose, for instance, that after a scrum a fly-half attempts a drop kick at goal and an opposing flanker – miles offside – bats the ball away. If the referee reckons the drop kick would probably have been successful, he gives a dropped goal.

The archives of my society – the Bristol Referees Society, probably the best in the world – contain a report of a penalty kick at goal during which a defender leaped so high that he managed to reach over the cross-bar and punch the ball back into the field-of-play. Intentional knock-on, of course. The referee, without hesitation, awarded the goal. A fine leap, nevertheless.

A kick at goal can also be *legally* deflected. It has been known for a player to hook his kick so ferociously that the ball set off towards a corner flag. The player turned away in disgust, and so failed to see the ball connect with a defender's head and ricochet over the cross-bar. Not a great goal, but a goal all the same.

No dummying the kick

If a player pretends to take a conversion kick but in fact doesn't, so that defenders charge too soon, the referee will allow them to go on charging. Same applies to free kicks and penalty kicks not taken at goal. If you dummy the kick in order to con your opponents and win another penalty, the referee will let play continue and you'll have to take the consequences.

Use the same ball

For a conversion kick or a penalty kick at goal, the kicker must use the ball that was in play. He can tee it up on sand or sawdust or a plastic tee if he likes.

Charge! (But do it quietly)

A defender must not charge a penalty kick. He can charge a conversion kick; as soon as the kicker begins his run or starts to kick, a defender can charge or jump or both. If the kicker is slow enough and the defender is fast enough, the defender might even charge down the kick, or at least take the kicker's eye off the ball. What defenders must not do is shout (or whistle, or sing).

Readers write

V.J. of Aberavon writes: Last Saturday, I kicked the ball over the goal-line, me and an opponent both dived for it, and I definitely got my hand to it first, but the bloody ref wouldn't give me the try.

D.R. Did you press down on the ball?

V.J. I definitely touched it first.

D.R. When you're not holding the ball – no downward pressure, no try.

V.J. You bloody refs are all alike.

D.R. I certainly hope so. And another thing: if the referee couldn't see you ground the ball, perhaps because other players were diving on it, he can't give the try.

V.J. That's scandalous.

D.R. That's life.

* * *

N.J.S. of Buenos Aires writes: I know the goal-posts are in the in-goal, but what about the protective post pads? Can you score a try against a post pad? Some are very thick.

D.R. They are still part of the goalposts. So the answer's yes.

* * *

W.W of West Hartlepool writes: I understand the momentum try, where you take the tackler with you. How about a sort of skate-over try, where the ball-carrier hasn't been tackled and he dives on to a big wet patch of mud that's short of the in-goal, so as to skid over the goal-line?

D.R. What's the advantage?

W.W. Makes it very hard for a tackler to stop him.

D.R. So what's your point?

W.W. Well, the tackle law says a player who goes to ground with the ball must immediately get up or let go of it, doesn't it?

D.R. True. But this skid-over happens in a flash, doesn't it?

W.W. How long is a flash? You'd be surprised how far some players can slide. It rains a lot up here.

* * *

G.D.L. of London writes: What you said about a player tackled just short of the line and reaching out to score, that's nothing new. There was a big debate about it at a meeting of the London Society of Referees in 1920.

D.R. What did they decide?

G.D.L. They said it was a try. By a majority vote.

D.R. Nothing changes.

* * *

C.J. of St. Ives writes: Just before the kick-off, our goal-posts got blown skew-whiff by the wind, so they looked like a letter H leaning sideways.

D.R. Italic.

C.J. If you say so. Anyway, I took a kick at goal and if the posts had been upright I'd have scored. But they weren't, and I didn't, so we lost.

D.R. That's tragic.

* * *

L.G. of Coventry writes: What's all the fuss about the rush of penalty tries? An attacking team takes a tapped penalty on their opponents' 5-metre line, they get nowhere because defenders simply stay offside and block the attack, the ref penalises this with another kick in exactly the same place – or a third, fourth, or fifth kick. He's wasting his breath!

D.R. Let's look at the law. A penalty try isn't an easy decision. Would the attackers *probably* have scored, but for foul play? Remember, offside is not foul play.

L.G. No, but intentionally offending is. So is repeatedly offending. They're professional fouls. If players won't respect the ref's big stick, they force him to reach for an even bigger stick. Otherwise he may as well go home.

D.R. You're right. The International Board "fully supports referees in the strict and uniform enforcement of the Laws as to repeated infringement". In senior matches, the IB says the referee "should always apply a strict standard". It says that "on the third occasion a caution must be given". It says that if he's unsure as to the balance of probability, he should give the benefit of the doubt to the non-offending team and award the penalty try.

13
Kicks

Kick-off

The game starts, and re-starts after half-time, with a place kick at the centre of the half-way line. After every score, play re-starts with a drop-kick taken on or behind the centre spot.

Who kicks off?

A toss-up before the match decides who kicks off. The winner can *either* choose which end he wants to defend *or* take the kick-off. If he prefers to choose ends, his opponents take the kick-off; if he wants the kick-off, his opponents choose ends.

Naturally, after half-time, when they change ends, the other side kicks off; and after a score it is always the side which has been scored against that kicks off.

It may come as a surprise to some people to learn that, strictly according to law, the captains actually perform the toss. I once refereed in Ireland, and the two captains gave me a very peculiar look when I offered them a coin before the match. Apparently it was the custom in those parts for the referee to spin the coin. Several interested spectators told me afterwards that, knowing those two fellahs, I was a lucky man to see my cash again.

What makes a good kick-off?

First, it must be in the right place: the centre of the half-way line for a place kick; on or just behind the centre for a drop-kick.

Second, it must be the right type of kick.

Third, the opposing team must stand at least ten metres from the half-way line.

Fourth, they must not charge until the ball has been kicked. Failing any of these conditions – if the kicker makes the wrong sort of kick, or the right kick in the wrong place; or if his opponents stand too near or charge too soon – the referee will order the kick to be taken again.

Fifth, the kicker's team must all be behind the ball. If the referee sees any of the kicker's team in front of the ball at the moment of kick-off, he orders a scrum at the centre.

Sixth, the ball must reach the ten metres line (a line ten metres from the half-way line and parallel to it) unless an opponent plays it first, in which case the game goes on. If it doesn't go far enough, the opponents can *either* have it kicked off again *or* take a scrum at

Kick-off from the centre. To start the match, and to restart it after half-time, the kick-off is a place kick from the centre spot. To restart play after a score, the kick-off is a drop kick from or behind the centre. The kicker's team must be behind the ball when kicked, and their opponents must be at least ten metres away. The ball should reach the ten-metre line and land in the field-of-play. If it fails to go ten metres but an opponent plays it first, then play goes on.

the centre. If it goes ten metres and the wind blows it back, play continues.

Seventh, the ball should land in the field-of-play. If it doesn't, what happens next depends on where it does land.

If the ball is kicked directly into touch, the other team has a three-way choice: either to have another kick-off, or to take a scrum at the centre, or to accept the kick and all that goes with it (which means a throw-in on the halfway line). If the ball is blown behind the halfway line and goes directly into touch, the throw-in is where it went into touch.

If the ball is kicked into the in-goal without touching a player on the way, the other team has a very different choice. They can either play on, or ground the ball, or make it dead by putting it into touch-in-goal or over the dead-ball line. Of course, it might go dead of its own accord, if it's travelling fast enough.

If they don't play on, they have yet another choice: either to have the ball kicked-off again, or to take a scrum at the centre. (They get the same choice if the kick-off sends the ball clean over the in-goal without even bouncing in it.)

Once a team has played on, they can't change their mind, ground the ball and ask for a scrum at the centre. When a defender runs with the ball or passes it, his team has played on. There's no going back.

This all makes sense. The purpose of the kick-off is to start the game in such a way that both sides have a fair chance of getting to the ball and doing something with it. By making one team stand back, and making the other team kick the ball to them, the laws create a situation in which anything could happen, and usually does.

If you're wondering what lies behind the option of a scrum-back at the centre after a kick-off that was grounded in the in-goal, I'll tell you. Not long ago, a kind of sleeping sickness had infected the game. The kick-off always went deep into the in-goal, the defending team always grounded the ball, and (under the old law) they restarted play with a 22 drop-out, which was what their opponents wanted. This dreary exchange guaranteed that, three seconds after the game began, the game stopped. The whole thing was a monumental yawn, until the lawmakers stepped in and put a sock in it. Now, any team that kicks off too deep finds itself rapidly back where it started; so it doesn't.

Drop-out

Apart from the special case I've just described, if the ball crosses a goal line and is made dead there, play restarts *either* with a five-metre scrum *or* with a drop-out, depending on several things which you can read all about in the chapter on the in-goal.

A drop-out is a drop-kick by the defending side, taken anywhere on or behind their 22-metre line. This line separates the two teams.

Up to this point, a drop-out is very like a kick-off: if the kicker makes the wrong sort of kick, or kicks from the wrong place, or if his opponents charge over the line too soon, the referee will whistle and order the kick to be taken again. And if any of the kicker's team is in front of the ball when it's kicked, the referee will order a scrum at the centre of the line. However, if they are in front of the ball because the kick was taken quickly, the referee will not stop play –

The 22 drop-out. The kick must be a drop-kick. It can be taken anywhere on or behind the 22-metre line. The kicker's team must be behind the ball when kicked, and their opponents must be on the other side of the line. The ball should cross the line and land in the field-of-play. Penalty for delay: free kick.

provided they keep retiring and stay out of the game until put onside by a team-mate.

Like the kick-off, a drop-out must go far enough but not too far. The ball must cross the 22-metre line; if it doesn't, the other team can either have the ball dropped out again or take a scrum at the centre of the line. (If the ball crosses the line and the wind blows it back, play goes on.) The ball should pitch inside the field-of-play. If it doesn't, the other side can either have another drop-out, or a scrum at the centre of the line, or accept the kick (which means taking a throw-in where the ball went into touch). All this, of course, follows the pattern of the kick-off.

Penalty kick

A penalty kick is a kick given to one side because the other side has done something seriously wrong.

The side that has been penalised has to (a) hand over the ball, and (b) clear off quickly. Temporarily, the game becomes very one-sided. That is the penalty for doing things that are penalised with penalty kicks.

As soon as the referee has given your opponents a penalty kick, you must at once run – not walk, but run – to a line ten metres behind the mark for the kick, or to your own goal line, whichever is the nearer. You can go further if you want to; but you must, if you can, give the other side at least ten metres of green grass in which to do their stuff. I don't know what you did to deserve all this, but let it be a lesson to you.

If you don't get back ten metres, or if you don't move fast enough, or if you deliberately put the ball out of your opponents' reach, or if you backchat, the referee will penalise you again by awarding a second penalty kick, ten metres in front of the first. (This second kick replaces the first. It must not be taken until the referee has made the mark for it – a slight pause which gives the penalised team time to retire.) And if you keep asking for trouble, he can shunt you back, ten metres at a time, until the mark is only five metres from your goal line.

That is the closest a penalty kick can be to the opponents' goal-line: five metres. When the offence takes place *less* than five metres

Beating retreat. Part of the penalty of a penalty kick is that you have to give the other team a clear ten metres in which to do what they like with the ball. As soon as the referee gives them a penalty kick, you must run ten metres from the mark towards your own goal line, or to that line if it's nearer.

from the line, the mark for the kick is always given on the five-metre line. This is to prevent the kind of situation where, with only inches separating the penalty kicker from the line, sheer brawn is bound to score.

So the situation is this. You have given them the ball, the foreground and the initiative. Can things get worse? Yes, they can.

Kick taken quickly

You, as the guilty team, must retreat immediately, but your opponents need not wait for you to do so. They can take a quick kick and attack. Even if some of their players are in front of the ball, the kicker is free to do his stuff. As long as they don't get involved in play, and they do their best to get onside, the game can carry on at high speed.

The scene at a quickly taken penalty kick may look thoroughly confused. You and your penalised team-mates are scrambling back ten metres. Some of your opponents are scrambling in the opposite direction, to get behind the ball. Simultaneously, the kicker – reckoning that the best time to attack is when you are completely disorganised – takes a tapped penalty and accelerates forward. You

Penalty kick taken quickly: two-way traffic. A player can take a quick penalty even though some team-mates are offside, provided they are trying to get back onside. Meanwhile, their opponents must retire 10 metres from the mark, fast. In the picture, the White No. 9 takes a quick tapped penalty and runs ahead. Black opponents, retiring 10 metres and running in the same direction, cannot touch him. White players (1 and 3), running in the opposite direction to get onside, are also out of the game. Thus, briefly, the White No. 9 is surrounded by friends and enemies who can do nothing except run away from each other. However, the Black No. 6 has retired 10 metres and can now make a tackle.

may find yourself running alongside him, heading for your own goal line yet unable to lay a finger on him.

This is because, even *after* the penalty kick is taken, you must keep retiring until you have covered ten metres or reached your goal line. The taking of the penalty kick does not put everybody back into the game. There is a terrible temptation to stop and see what's going on, because after all they *are* the enemy, and they *are* up to something. Resist it. The first thing you must do is retire ten metres. Your opponents may be launching the most dangerous attack, but there's nothing you can do about it until you've put yourself back into the game by retiring ten metres or to your own goal line – *with one exception*. If, while you are straining every nerve to retire ten metres and so on, a team-mate who was a least ten metres from the mark for the kick runs in front of you, this brings you back into the game. You can stop retiring and get stuck in again.

But it's worth understanding the full implications of this bit of law. For instance: suppose that when your team is penalised you are 15 metres nearer your opponents' goal line. This means you must retire a total of 25 metres (or to your own goal line) before you can rejoin the game – unless, of course, a team-mate runs forward and puts you onside. Meanwhile your opponents are on the attack. Several may have handled the ball by the time you catch up. You're keen to tackle. Don't do it. Don't do anything, until you've done what the law requires.

Penalty round-up

A penalty kick can be of any kind – place, drop or punt – and any player can take it. The kicker can use a placer to hold the ball, if he wants. He must not place-kick for touch. The kick must be made either on or behind the mark, which the referee indicates with a delicate bash from his heel. Pay attention to that mark, and be sure you make your kick somewhere on a line through it. If the referee makes his mark *here*, and you gallop up, all a-twitter with impatience, and take the kick *there*, five metres to the right, he'll blow up, recall the ball, and give a scrum, opponents' put-in.

You can take a penalty kick anywhere behind the mark, on a line through it and parallel with the touch-lines. This allows you to adjust the angle to improve your chances of a kick at goal. You can even go as far back as your own in-goal if you want to (I can't see what good it would do). If you take a penalty kick inside your in-goal and the ball goes into touch-in-goal or over the dead-ball line, the referee orders a five-metre scrum, attacking team's put-in.

Apart from this, you're free to kick the ball in any direction, and any player – including the kicker – can play it next. Mind you, a penalty kick must be a *kick*. Bouncing the ball on your knee is not a kick. Tapping it on your toe is not a kick. Knocking it with your heel is not a kick. A kick is only a kick if you hit the ball with your foot, or your leg below the knee, hard enough to send it out of your hands (if you're holding it) or away from the mark (if it's on the ground). It doesn't have to go far but it must go somewhere. More important, the referee must see that it has gone somewhere. If you turn your back on the referee and fumble with the ball, don't be surprised if he calls play back and orders a scrum; he's not clairvoyant, you know. Do the obvious thing: let him *watch* you taking the penalty kick. Then he can see what's happened.

Penalty kick at goal

Once you've let the referee know that you're going to take a penalty kick at goal, you're committed to it. You must go for goal; if you try anything else the referee will disallow the kick and give a scrum. And there are more ways of letting the referee know than spitting on the ball and mumbling something about having a bash. If you start placing the ball as if for a kick at goal, squinting at the uprights, tossing little bits of grass into the wind, and so on, this says irrevocably that you are going for goal, and it's no good whispering huskily to him that really you're not. He may even ask you what you plan to do; he has the right.

The reason is simple. If you are taking a kick at goal, he will send the touch-judges around behind the posts. If you're not, he'll leave them where they are more use. What he *won't* stand for is sending the touch-judges behind the posts and then seeing you kick the ball into touch.

If you don't let the referee know that you intend to kick at goal, and then you take a drop kick and it goes over, this is a goal. It just

Penalty kick at goal. This can be taken anywhere on a line through the mark for the kick, so the kicker can go back to improve his angle. Defenders must retire at least ten metres from the mark (or to their goal line if it's nearer) and they must stand still, arms by their sides, while the kick is being taken.

means that you've done it without benefit of touch-judges.

As with kick-offs and drop-outs and conversions, all the kicker's team (except the placer, if one is used) must be behind the ball when it's kicked. Otherwise the referee will give a scrum at the mark.

You are not obliged to accept a penalty kick, by the way. You can have a scrum at the mark, if you'd rather. Up to you.

Drop kick

You make a drop kick by letting the ball fall to the ground from your hands and kicking it on the first rebound. The only times when you *must* drop-kick the ball are when making a drop-out, when making a kick-off after a score, and when attempting a dropped goal. Otherwise you might as well punt.

In the early days of the game, most kicks were drop kicks. As late as the 1860s spectators booed punting; but the ball was a slightly different shape then. The oval leather case was filled with an inflated pig's bladder, and this usually made the ends well rounded. The ball was more suited to place-kicking and drop-kicking than today's relatively pointed ball, which is shaped for handling as well as kicking. Of course, a hundred years ago many people thought there was far too much handling in rugby too.

Free kick

There is only one sort of free kick, but there are two reasons for giving it. *Either* it's a kick awarded to one team because of an offence by the other team, *or* it's a kick which a player earns by making a fair-catch, or 'Mark!'.

A free kick can be a place, punt or drop, but you cannot place-kick to touch with a free kick. You cannot score a goal from a free kick. If you prefer, you can take a scrum instead of a free kick.

Free kick from a fair-catch, or 'Mark!'

A fair catch gives you a chance to stop the game temporarily in order to protect yourself when you're catching the ball from an opponent's kick.

Mark! or Fair-Catch. To claim a fair-catch, you must do three things, all at once – catch the ball cleanly; be in or behind your 22; and shout 'Mark!' Get it right and the referee will award you a free kick.

To make a fair catch you must do three things, all at the same time:

1 Catch the ball cleanly, direct from an opponent's kick (but not including a kick-off).
2 Be in your 22-metre area or your in-goal.
3 Shout 'Mark!'

This feat isn't easy, especially when the ball is coming out of the sun and the earth is trembling beneath the pounding hooves of hungry opponents. The usual time to make a fair-catch is when your team is in deep trouble and you need a break, so by definition you're under pressure. Nevertheless, you must bring off all three parts perfectly, and all together. If you catch the ball and then drop it, or if you knock-on and make a second catch, or if you're outside your 22, or if you shout the magic word too late – it's no good. The referee won't whistle, and it's no use giving him that long, reproachful stare.

Robinson's First Law of Rugby says that, when a law is changed, it always takes at least ten years for the old version to fade away. Long ago, when you claimed a fair-catch you had to make a mark with your heel as you shouted 'Mark!' Occasionally today you can see veteran players still denting the turf in that old-fashioned way as they field a kick. More recently, the fair-catch law was changed so that the player need not have both feet on the ground at the crucial moment. Now even that has been abolished. Now he can jump and claim a fair-catch while he's off the ground entirely. No doubt the traditionalists will stand firm on both feet as they make their mark, for a long time to come.

You can make a fair-catch on the run and when you've done it you shouldn't hang around. Your opponents won't wait for the whistle, and neither should you. Beat it fast, while your legs still function. If the referee allows your fair-catch you haven't lost anything, and if he doesn't, then you're going to have to do something in a hurry anyway.

You can make a fair-catch in your own in-goal, and you can make one after the ball has bounced off a goal post or cross-bar.

Making a fair-catch entitles you to a free kick. Only the player who made the fair-catch can take the free kick. If he's injured there's a scrum at the mark instead, with his team putting in the ball. And if he made his fair-catch in his in-goal, the scrum goes down five metres from the goal-line, opposite the mark.

Free kick following an offence

Unlike the 'fair-catch' free kick, this free kick can be awarded anywhere in the field-of-play and it can be taken by any player in the team.

The free kick: full description

A free kick has a lot in common with a penalty kick. A free kick must be taken at the mark or anywhere behind it on a line through the mark, parallel with touch. If the kick has been awarded for an offence within five metres of the opponents' goal-line, the mark is made five metres out from that goal-line. The kick must be taken without undue delay. All the kicker's team must be behind the ball (except a placer to hold a place kick). The kick must noticeably move the ball, either out of the kicker's hands or away from the mark on the ground. The kicker is free to kick the ball in any direction and he can play it again if he wishes.

The big difference between a free kick and a penalty kick lies in its scoring power (none) and in the fact that the opposing side is allowed to charge it.

A team awarded a free kick cannot score a dropped goal until after an opponent has played the ball, or after an opponent has made a tackle, or after a maul has formed, or after the ball is dead. A lot to remember.

As soon as a free kick is awarded, the other team must immediately run until they are ten metres behind the mark or they have reached their own goal line – just as for a penalty kick. They must keep running, even after the free kick has been taken, until they've covered ten metres or until an onside team-mate runs in front of them. And – just as with a penalty kick – a team awarded a free kick need not wait until all its players are behind the ball. If the kick is taken so quickly that some team-mates are offside, they won't be penalised as long as they take no part in the game and they retire at once. This is all very familiar.

Unlike a penalty kick, however, a free kick can be charged, and even charged down. Once the other team has retreated ten metres, their beady little eyes will be fixed on the kicker and their feet will be pawing the ground, just itching for him to make a move. The instant the kicker starts his run or offers to kick, they can hurl themselves at him. He can't afford to waver or feint and then draw back. Once he's made a move his opponents will be after him, and if he hesitates they may well succeed in preventing him from taking the kick altogether. That means a scrum at the mark, their put-in.

Now that you see what a difference a good charge can make, you'll understand why the laws insist that the kicker makes a definite kick, moving the ball unmistakeably out of his hands or along the ground, even if it only goes a matter of inches; and why rubbing the ball on the toecap is not enough. The other team must be able to tell when they're entitled to charge.

There's no doubt about the start of the kicker's run; but if the kicker takes a tapped kick, it must be a clear and visible signal to everyone, including the enemy. (The same is true of the penalty kick. Although the other team must not move *until* a penalty kick has been taken, they're free to rush in all directions *as soon as* it's taken, so it's essential that they should know exactly when that moment is.)

If the other team fails to get back ten metres quickly enough, or if they charge too soon, the referee will cancel the free kick and give a second free kick, ten metres forward (not to be taken until he's made the mark). Any player may take this kick. And if they do something gormless like throwing the ball over the hedge, he might well regard that as misconduct and award a penalty kick.

Readers write

B.M. of Llanelli writes: I still reckon you should be able to kick a goal from a free kick.

D.R. Forget it. You're history.

* * *

P.Z. of Bucharest writes: This business about a team being free to take a quick penalty kick is all very well, but what if the ref wants to warn an opponent for his foul play? The ref's standing and talking, while they're off and running.

D.R. You're right. Yet another dilemma for the referee. It's a tough job.

14
The in-goal

The in-goal is the area behind the goal-line. It is bordered by the goal-line, which is part of the in-goal. If the ball lands on the goal line, play goes on (unless a try is scored). The rest of the in-goal is bordered by the touch-in-goal lines and the dead-ball line. They are not part of the in-goal. If the ball touches them, or anything or anyone beyond them, it's dead.

The great attraction of the in-goal is that it's the only place where you can score a try or make a touch-down. Apart from that – and the fact that scrums, rucks, mauls, line-outs and tackles can't take place there – the in-goal is just like the field-of-play. A knock-on in an in-goal is still a knock-on; a player who is offside in an in-goal can get into trouble just as easily as if he were in midfield. Nearly all the laws apply behind the goal-line just as they do in front of it.

But although the game is much the same, the consequences are not. The referee's decision varies according to which team did what, and where.

Drop-out

If an attacking player puts or takes the ball into his opponents' in-goal and it becomes dead there, the result is a drop-out.

This does not include the situation where an attacker knocks-on or throws-forward in the field-of-play so that the ball goes into the in-goal and it's made dead there. In that case, the referee orders a scrum where the knock-on or throw-forward happened.

It does include the situation where a defender's kick is charged down by an attacking player in the field-of-play and the ball goes into the in-goal.

What matters is the fact that an attacking player's action sent the ball into the in-goal. It makes no difference if the ball touched a defender before it crossed the goal line, provided he didn't try to play the ball.

So the drop-out law is simple. If an attacker – without breaking a law – sends the ball into his opponents' in-goal, and anyone makes it dead (not including a try), the defending team gets a drop-out. (Made dead in in-goal direct from a kick-off is different; see *kick-off*.)

What's more, if an attacker boots the ball into his opponents' in-goal and his kick makes it dead in touch-in-goal or over the dead-ball line, his opponents get a choice – either a drop-out, or a scrum where the ball was kicked. Reason? To discourage delaying tactics, and keep the ball in play.

For the purposes of this law, 'made dead' means a defender grounded the ball (touch-down) or any player put it into touch-in-goal or over the dead-ball line. It doesn't mean a try was scored.

Foiled pushover. Once the ball in a scrum reaches or crosses the goal line, the scrum has ended and anyone can ground the ball – including (as shown here) the defending scrum-half. Result: touch-down and (because the attacking team took the ball into the in-goal) a drop-out.

Five-metre scrum

This is a scrum on the defending team's five-metre line, and it's even simpler than the drop-out law, because a five-metre scrum is awarded on every other occasion when the ball is made dead in or beyond the in-goal. If the ball's dead and it's not a drop-out, it must be a five-metre scrum. Unless the attacking team infringed a law in some way, they always get the put-in.

To sum up: a ball made dead after an attacker put it into the in-goal (without offending) means a drop-out. A ball made dead after a defender put it into the in-goal means a five-metre scrum. Is that really all there is to it? Well, almost.

A five-metre scrum usually comes about because a defending player took or put the ball into his in-goal and couldn't get it out again, so he was obliged to make it dead. (Known as 'minoring' in some parts of the world.) But the in-goal can be a hectic place. What happens if a player – either a defender or an attacker – has the ball in an in-goal, and his opponents have such a grip of him that he can't ground it? He's what's known as 'held up in the in-goal' and the referee orders a five-metre scrum, attackers' put-in. Same applies if the referee can't decide which team first grounded the ball, as sometimes happens when opposing players dive on it. And in both these cases, it makes no difference which team originally took the ball into the in-goal: it's always a five-metre scrum, and it's always the attackers' put-in.

What happens when a scrum or a ruck gets pushed into an in-goal and a defender grounds the ball? Well, it depends. If the defending team was in possession at the time – that is, the ball was in their half of the scrum or ruck as it got rumbled over the goal line – then a five-metre scrum is formed. But if the attacking team was in possession but a defender managed to poach a touch-down first, the outcome is a drop-out. I've seen it happen. The attacking team bust a gut in an effort to get a pushover try, and just as their No. 8 dribbled the ball onto the goal line, the opposing scrum-half dived in and whacked the ball with his hand. Smart play, and well worth the drop-out it earned.

Lastly, an oddity. If a defending team takes a free kick or a penalty kick in their in-goal, and they cock it up so that the ball is made dead before it can cross the goal line, the consequence is a five-metre scrum, attacking team's put-in.

Errors in the in-goal

You can knock-on or throw-forward in an in-goal just as easily as in the field-of-play. If the referee's any good, he'll wait for a second or two before he blows up, in case the other team can take advantage of your mistake. If there's no advantage, he'll give a five-metre scrum, opposite the place where you went wrong. And if you're an attacking player, this is the one case where the defending team gets the put-in at a five-metre scrum.

You can be offside in an in-goal. Easily. After all, the space may be up to 22 metres deep: plenty of room for you to stray in front of a team-mate who has the ball or who has just kicked it, and then to interfere with play. In fact, most of the offences that happen in the field-of-play can also happen in the in-goal. Not the tackle offences, nor the scrum/ruck/maul offences, because those events are confined to the field-of-play. But the Foul Play law certainly applies to the in-goal. Punching, charging, kicking, tripping and any other kind of dangerous or unfair play will get you penalised, and – as usual – the referee can warn a player or send him off. The referee can always award a penalty try if he thinks that foul play prevented a probable try; equally, he can disallow a try if he thinks foul play by an attacker contributed to it.

So any action (foul play, offside, whatever) that deserves a free kick or a penalty kick if it happens in the field-of-play gets just the same treatment when it's done in an in-goal – with one big difference. The mark for a free kick or a penalty kick can never be in an in-goal. The mark must always be in the field-of-play. Where exactly, depends on whether the ball was in play or out of play at the time of the crime.

For any offence in an in-goal while the ball is in play, the kick is awarded on the five-metre line. If an attacker was guilty, the defending team get the kick and probably boots the ball into touch. If a defender was guilty, the attacking team gets the kick. As they can take the ball back from the mark, they might well attempt a penalty goal.

Misconduct while the ball is out of play is different. Dirty work in an in-goal when the ball is dead – I leave the grubby details to your steamy imagination – results in a penalty kick being awarded where the ball would next have been brought into play. That could be on the five-metre line (instead of a five-metre scrum), or on the 22 (instead of a drop-out), or at the centre spot (after a try). So it's conceivably possible for a team to score a try, then commit misconduct in the in-goal, then attempt the conversion kick, and *then* have to face a penalty kick by their opponents from the centre spot.

There's one exception. It applies to the offence of intentionally obstructing an opponent in the in-goal when he's just kicked the ball. I think we can safely assume that this opponent is a defender. His team can choose to take a penalty kick *either* on their five-metre line *or* where the ball landed. If it came down in or near touch, leave it to the ref to sort out.

Fine tuning

A five-metre scrum is always awarded opposite the place where the knock-on or throw-forward happened or where the ball was made dead. The scrum must be at least five metres from a touch line. The attacking team always puts in the ball, unless they made the knock-on or throw-forward.

When a free kick or penalty kick is awarded on the five-metre line, the mark for the kick is opposite the place of the offence. When the kick is awarded instead of a drop-out, it can be taken anywhere on the 22-metre line. When it's awarded on the centre spot it's taken on the centre spot, which is so obvious that I wonder why I bother.

Last word

There can be no rucks or mauls in the in-goal, remember. This is one of the few laws which don't apply there. Another is the tackle, legally speaking. Tackles – as the law defines them – cannot happen in an in-goal, which is not to say that you can't grab an opponent who has the ball there. You can, and as there are no mauls, legally speaking, in the in-goal, other defenders can converge from all sides to help hold him up. Result: stalemate, which the referee breaks with his famous five-metre scrum.

Readers write

M.M. of Essex writes: Someone told me that when Romania played Wales, in September 1994, Wales scored ten points without a Romanian player touching the ball. How?

D.R. Simple. Try plus conversion plus penalty goal equals ten points. Immediately after a Welsh player scored a try, a Romanian player fell on him and jabbed him in the back with his elbow. That's misconduct while the ball is out of play, so the kick was awarded where the game would have restarted, and Wales kicked the penalty from the halfway line.

* * *

B.R. of Sydney writes: I've been thinking about what you said to V.J. of Aberavon at the end of the chapter on scoring. Several players dive on the ball, the referees can't see who grounded it, so he can't give the try, you said.

D.R. Correct. Good refs never guess.

B.R. But you never said what he does next.

D.R. You're right, I didn't. It's a 5-metre scrum. Any time the referee has doubts about grounding in the in-goal, it's always a 5-metre scrum, attacking team's put-in.

15
Advantage

The Advantage Law is the best law in the book, because it lets you ignore all the others for the good of the game. It goes like this.

When one side breaks a law, and the other side gains an advantage from this, the referee lets the game go on.

For example: if a player knocks on but an opponent intercepts the ball and makes good use of it, the referee will gladly forget about the knock-on. And the advantage gained doesn't have to be territorial; it can be tactical. Take the same example again: if the opponent who snapped up the knock-on found himself about to be tackled, he obviously couldn't hope to make much ground, so territorial advantage is out. On the other hand, he might have an unmarked team-mate outside him, just waiting to take a pass; in which case there would be a good chance of tactical advantage.

Now, perhaps, you see why people are always urging you to play to the whistle. It isn't just that the referee might have missed the knock-on (which you saw so clearly and slowed down because of). It's far more likely that he saw the knock-on *and waited to see if it gave any advantage to the other side.* For the referee, as we have discovered already, is not clairvoyant; the only way he can find out if you are smart enough to exploit your opponents' mistakes is by giving you the chance.

Therefore, he must let play go on for a couple of seconds after the infringement, before he can decide whether or not an advantage has been gained. If you hesitate about grabbing an opportunity because you think the whistle *should* have gone, you defeat the whole purpose of the advantage law, which is to *keep the game going.* Let the referee look after the mistakes; your job is to get the ball and score. The referee will do all he can to leave these opportunities open to you, but only you can take advantage of them.

And if it turns out that you don't in fact get any advantage from whatever it was, he'll bring back play and award you the scrum or the kick. So you can't lose.

The advantage law covers ninety-nine per cent of the game. Virtually every time your opponents go wrong, you can profit from it. Advantage covers scrums, rucks, mauls, line-outs, knock-ons, forward passes, free kicks, tackles, drop-outs, in-goal play, and all kinds and conditions of offside. There are a million ways you can use advantage, and the referee will be looking for them all.

Exceptions. Only five parts of the game are *not* covered by advantage. They are:

1 When the ball or a player carrying it touches the referee.
2 When a scrum is wheeled through more than 90 degrees.
3 When a scrum collapses.
4 When a player in a scrum is lifted off his feet or forced upwards out of the scrum.

Territorial advantage: gain in ground. This little scenario happens all the time. The Black player gets a pass, knocks it on, and an opponent smartly boots the ball past him. This is territorial advantage. The referee lets play go on. If Whites get no advantage (for instance, if another Black catches the kick-ahead) the referee orders a scrum where the knock-on happened.

5   When the ball comes out of either end of the tunnel at a scrum
    without having been played.

That last item raises several interesting points which I've already
kicked around in the chapter on scrums, so I shan't repeat them
here. I just want to add the obvious fact that although advantage
may not always apply to the way the ball comes out of the tunnel, it
certainly does apply to the way it goes into the tunnel. If the scrum-
half, in a fit of absentmindedness, puts the ball in crookedly under
the opposing hooker's feet, the referee should let him get on with it.

The same thing applies to line-outs. The thrower is supposed to
throw the ball in straight, but if his unstraight throw favours his
opponents, why stop the game?

*Tactical advantage: good possession. At a scrum near Whites' goal line, Blacks win
the ball. A White flanker (No. 6) breaks too soon and is caught offside. However,
Blacks have good possession and they're in a good position to take tactical
advantage, so the referee lets play go on. If Blacks' attack comes to nothing, he goes
back and penalises the White flanker. So Blacks can't lose. Note that the ball is still
in the scrum. The Black scrum-half is waiting for it to come out before he grabs it.*

And if, at a drop-out, the ball goes backwards instead of forwards and the other side is waiting for it when it comes down, good luck to them. Also full advantage.

Consider a scrum near the posts. As the attacking side heels the ball a defending flanker is caught offside. Should the referee immediately blow up? Not necessarily. The attacking team might get a try and convert it: seven points, against three for a penalty goal. So, while making it clear that he has seen the offside offence, the referee can let the attack develop. If it fails, he can still award the penalty kick for offside.

One of the biggest idiots in rugby is the player who keeps reminding the referee when something has gone wrong. He thinks he sees a knock-on, so he shouts 'Knock-on!'. This is stupid, because:

1 the referee, being human, resents being told what to do, and
2 he's playing advantage and trying *not* to stop the game, while this pessimist has never heard of advantage and spends his afternoon *looking* for reasons to stop the game.

The advantage law is a splendid idea. It makes playing a pleasure and refereeing an art. It is beautifully simple: when in doubt, play on! As Milton* once said, 'Advantage is the oil that greases the gears of the game,' and he should know. In rugby, as in life, one man's grief is another man's gravy.

* Cedric McGregor Milton, famed Manx referee.

Readers write

P.R.A. of Middlesex writes: When the referee plays advantage, how far should he let play continue before he either forgets the offence or brings play back?

D.R. How long is a broken bootlace? It's up to him to decide how long is long enough. Territorial advantage is fairly easy to measure. Tactical advantage is harder. Are you talking about time or distance?

P.R.A. Both.

D.R. I've seen a top-class referee play advantage for a knock-on at a line-out that resulted in the ball going all along the backline until the winger got tackled into touch on the far side of the field, and that referee then brought the teams back and gave a scrum at the place of the line-out. So he played advantage for about 70 metres. As for time: I reckon that if a team takes advantage of a minor infringement, and is checked, and wins quick second-phase possession, and attacks again, then they've had plenty of benefit from the advantage and the referee can forget about the infringement. If it was a serious offence, such as Foul Play, he would never forget about it. All this is just my opinion. Each referee must decide the case on its merits.

* * *

T.A. of Somerset writes: If a player shouts 'Knock-on, ref!' I reckon the ref should blow up. Any player with a mouth that big doesn't deserve advantage.

D.R. A friend of mine refereed a match in which a player kept on pointing out everything that went wrong. Then his team took advantage of an opponent's offence in their 22, ran the ball 80 yards and scored. Before he blew his whistle, the referee said to this player, 'Of course, you can always have the scrum back in your 22, if you'd prefer it.' He shut up after that.

16
Loose ends

What you can't wear

The law about what you can and cannot wear has been considerably tightened up. This is because players have been seen wearing bullet-proof corsets, and headgear like boxers' sparring helmets, and jerseys with shoulders that reach their ears. These are all banned.

Some padding is allowed. You can wear shoulder pads provided they cover only the shoulder and the collarbone, and are no thicker than one centimetre when uncompressed (including any straps or containers). Same applies to scrumcaps. One centimetre is three-eights of an inch.

You can wear elasticated supports (like cycling shorts) but they must be washable. Padded shorts are banned. So is any bloodstained clothing. You can wear bandages or dressings to cover an injury; tape for support or to prevent an injury; shinpads and ankle supports (which must be under a sock); mitts (but not gloves). There's an obvious ban on buckles, clips, rings, zippers, and the like; and a general ban on any item (apart from shoulder pads and scrumcaps) more than half a centimetre thick, and made of a hard material. (What does 'hard' mean? It means a density of more than 45kg per cubic metre. I bet you're sorry you asked.) So any clothing more than half a centimetre (three-sixteenths of an inch) thick is banned.

Studs must be of regulation size, carry the kite mark, and not have sharp edges. A single stud in the toe of the boot is illegal.

(Moulded-rubber-studded boots are allowed.) Finally there's a catch-all bit of law that says the referee can ban any item of clothing if he thinks it's liable to injure any player. And if, before the match, the referee tells a player something's illegal, and then finds he's wearing it on the field of play, that's an offence under the law of Unfair Play, and he gets sent off.

How long is a match?

Maximum playing time in a match is 80 minutes. Internationals and other top matches always last 80 minutes. Lower down the game there's no set time, and the two teams can decide how long they want to play. Failing that, the referee decides. There's no minimum time, but play must be split into halves, and after half-time the teams must change ends. Players and officials may leave the field at half-time, if they wish. The half-time interval is ten minutes at the most, and if both teams dislike standing about in the pouring rain they can scrub round the interval and kick off as soon as they've sucked their bits of orange; or sooner.

Some games may go on after the end of the second half: these are drawn matches in a knock-out competition for which the Union has authorised extra time to be played if necessary. Extra time must not be played in Under-19 matches. On the other hand some matches may stop before the end of the second half: the referee has power to call a halt at any time if he believes that the match cannot be completed (because of fog, say, or a blizzard) or if he reckons it would be dangerous to carry on playing.

Leaving and entering the field

Except at half-time, you (or your team) cannot leave the playing enclosure to change jerseys – unless a jersey's become bloodstained, in which case it *must* be changed. If you want to leave the field-of-play for any reason, you must get the referee's permission. Similarly, you must not come back until he allows it, which he will do only when the ball is dead. A friend of mine was refereeing a fairly non-vintage match with more than its fair share of thud and blunder, when two large players began fighting. They lurched over the touch line, still swinging haymakers, but he ignored them and let play continue. When they realised that nobody was paying any attention, they gradually stopped fighting and turned towards the field-of-play. He told them to stay where they were. They had left the playing enclosure without his permission, he said, and according to law they must not return until he gave them permission to do so, which certainly wasn't going to happen in a hurry. Five minutes later he let them come back. From then on, he said, it was a much better game. He bent the law a little. However, he certainly made it fit the needs of the moment.

Throughout a match – and that includes half-time – nobody is allowed on the playing area unless the referee says so. If he lets anyone come onto the field it's only briefly. As soon as they've done what they came to do – treat an injury, for example – they go off again. At half-time, the referee will allow the coach of each team onto the field to tell them what's going wrong. Then they, too, must disappear.

When does the match end?

Unlike soccer – where, believe it or not, the final whistle can blow while the ball is in mid-air, *en route* from boot to goal – each half of a game of rugby can end only when the ball is dead. Even then, the game may not be over. If time runs out after the referee has awarded a scrum, a line-out, a try, a penalty kick or a free kick, then play goes on until the ball next becomes dead. Normal playing time is up, but the scrum or line-out takes place, or the scoring team tries to convert the try, or the penalty or free kick is taken. And in the case of the set-piece restarts or the last two kicks, play may well go on for some time. The losing team might even score, and win. Stranger things have happened.

How many players?

You can have any number of players up to a maximum of fifteen in each team. Fifteen is the customary number, and seems about right for this sort of game; but if you can't raise that many, it's perfectly legal to play with fewer, as countless Sevens Tournaments have proved.

Fifteen is an extraordinarily difficult number to count up to, involving as it does both hands and one foot; so it sometimes happens during a game that one team, finding itself constantly outnumbered, starts adding up its opponents and reaches the figure sixteen. If this occurs they're entitled to inform the referee, who will make the opposing captain get rid of one man; but he won't alter the score. Most referees check the teams before the kick-off anyway, and reduce the numbers if they're over the limit.

However, the referee is not obliged to do anything if a team has *fewer* than fifteen players – and it's amazing how many sides spend the first ten minutes of the match wondering why there's such a big hole in their defence, until they realise that their inside-centre is watching the women's hockey, two pitches away.

What if the ball touches the referee?

1 *In the field-of-play*. If the ball – or a player carrying it – touches the referee in the field-of-play and neither sides gains an advantage from this, he lets play go on. If he thinks one side *has* gained an advantage, he'll order a scrum on the spot. The team of the player who last had the ball will put it in.

2 *In the in-goal*. If the ball held by a player, or a player with the ball, touches the referee in an in-goal, and that player's team gains no advantage from this, he lets play go on. If an advantage is gained, he awards a try (if an attacking player had the ball) or a touch-down (if a defender had it) at the place where the player or the ball touched the referee.

   If the ball itself – not held by a player – touches the referee or a touch-judge or a spectator in an in-goal, the referee will whistle up at once and base his decision on what would probably have happened next. If he thought a defender would probably have got a touch-down or that the ball would otherwise have gone dead, he'll give a touch-down; if he thought an attacking player would probably have scored a try, he'll award a try.

   This is commonsense. Rugby is a fast-moving game. Occasionally the ball or the ball-carrier will touch the referee. As long as neither team benefits, there's no reason to stop play. But a loose ball in the in-goal: that's different.

Injury time and other delays

If you are injured, you are allowed up to one minute to recover. After that you must either get on or get off, always assuming that you *can* get off. If you can't, the referee will allow whatever time it takes to load you on to the stretcher. But for walking wounded, one minute each is the maximum delay. This time is always made up in the half when it was lost. If the referee has to stop play because of an injury, he restarts it with a scrum. The team last in possession of the ball gets the put-in.

Injury time is a privilege, not a right. The referee is not obliged to halt proceedings just because someone isn't feeling very well, and in any case he certainly won't interrupt play for injury if he thinks the damage is minor. What he will do is let the casualty lie in the mud, moaning piteously and twitching, while the action continues all around.

If somebody who's medically trained is available, the referee may let him or her come onto the field and treat a minor injury while play continues. When the ball is dead the referee will go over and look at the player, who has usually staged a miraculous recovery by then.

Referees take no risks in this area, especially in junior rugby; but they soon get to know the difference between a dislocated shoulder and the aftermath of ten pints of lager and a double vindaloo. I was refereeing a Sunday-morning match when a player got tackled, not very hard, and lay on his back, making peculiar noises. I waved play on. The rest of his team protested angrily. They claimed he was badly hurt. Eventually the ball went dead, and I went back and asked him what was wrong. 'Hangover,' he croaked. Then he threw up on his captain's boots and crawled off the field. I suppose it might have been a heart attack. But if the referee treated every winded player as if he were dying, the match would never end.

Furthermore, if the referee has reason to believe that a player's injury is bogus, that he's not really hurt at all, he can order him to be dumped outside the playing area so that everyone else can get on with the game.

Other delays which the referee may take into account are for things like lost balls, rabid dogs loose on the field, replacing the cross-bar (rare), re-erecting the goal posts (very rare), clothing the naked, searching for contact lenses, giving passage to livestock, and violent hailstorms (hen's-egg size and up). I remember a game where three minutes were added on for pushing the ambulance out of the mud. They couldn't leave it where it was: the bloke inside was bleeding all over the floor. Besides, the back wheels were right across the touch-in-goal line.

What the referee will not allow delays for are things like thirst*, legal dispute, tight boots, fatigue, blowing the nose, or waving to the girlfriend.

Bleeding wounds

A player who has an open or a bleeding wound must go off. He can't come back until it's been patched up or stitched up so that it's no longer leaking gore, and also covered up. Don't be fooled by that word 'wound'. A nose that's pouring blood is a bleeding wound, even though there's no broken skin to be seen.

Replacements and substitutes

A replacement is not the same as a substitute. A player can be replaced only for injury, and if that's no worse than a bleeding wound which can be treated and covered, then he can return to the game. There's nothing to stop a player coming on as a replacement more than once in a match; but he can come on as a substitute only once. A player can be substituted for any reason. Once that's done, he's off for good – with one small exception. A player who's been substituted may replace a blood injury or an injured front-row player if no suitably trained replacement is available.

If you find all this confusing, you're not alone. The fact is that each one of those players in tracksuits sitting on the bench is capable of being used either as a replacement or as a substitute. Indeed, he could be a temporary replacement (for a blood injury) and later a permanent substitute (for any reason at all). What's more, if he got a blood injury while playing as a substitute, he could be

---

* Water breaks are allowed in some countries.

temporarily replaced, get patched up, and return to the action. There is a lot of coming and going in modern rugby; so much so that in top matches the referee has the help of what's called a 'fourth official' to monitor and control changes in personnel.

Temporary versus permanent

Since all substitution is permanent while some replacement is temporary and some isn't, it's useful to know exactly how the system works. After all, a team might want its key player back in the game, even if he has lost some blood.

The only player who may be temporarily replaced – meaning that if he returns, his replacement leaves the field – is one with an open or bleeding wound. This is the only kind of injury which gets such special treatment. For instance, if a player twists an ankle (no broken skin, no blood), he can be replaced – but it must be a permanent replacement. His ankle might feel fine after a while. Tough luck. He can't come back.

There's a reason for this discrimination. A bleeding player has no choice. The referee orders him to go and get treatment. Other players with other injuries can decide for themselves whether to stay or go; and if a suffering player reckons the internal damage (no blood, remember) is so great that he needs replacing, then the laws reckon he's not fit to play again in that match.

Note that you can replace a replacement. If he too gets injured, you can bring on yet another player. It makes no difference to the status of the original bleeding player. If he can get repaired, he can return.

There's an interesting historical sidelight on the question of replacement. It involves the meaning of the word 'match'. A match was so-called because it was reckoned that the teams were matched: they were alike enough to make a good contest. In the early days of rugby they used to solve the whole problem of replacement by adopting what you might call 'reverse substitution'. Whenever an injured man had to go off, the captain of the *other* team sent off one of his men. This restored the balance and made it a true match once more. There have been worse ideas.

Concussion and other headaches

Normally, the best person to decide whether or not an injured player should go off is that player himself. Sometimes, however, the player cannot make that decision – for instance, if he's been concussed. If someone medically qualified advises that it would be dangerous for that player to stay in the game, or if the injury is obviously serious, the referee has the power to make him go off either for running repairs or for good. (And if he has been concussed, the International Board has laid down that he should not play or train for at least three weeks, and then only if a neurological examination has cleared him.)

At the very top level (such as international matches or matches involving a national representative team) the tricky question of whether or not a player is badly hurt has been taken out of the referee's hands. At that level, a doctor decides whether or not the injury is so bad that the player should not continue. Note that the question is not how *fit* the player is, but how damaging his injury is. The point of the replacement-for-injury law is to protect an injured player from aggravating the damage by playing on because he doesn't want to leave his team a man short. At all the top matches, the referee will get the advice of a doctor when a player is hurt. The first priority of the referee is the player's safety. If he thinks someone might be badly hurt, he'll stop play immediately – even if a team may be about to score a try.

The Cardiff Scenario

If a replacement for a blood injury gets sent off for Foul Play, that's bad news for the bleeding player. He can't return. He suffers for his team-mate's folly. But there's an interesting twist to the tale. A few years ago, in the middle of a Wales-England match, a Welsh prop got sent off. No other Welsh player on the field was competent to move into the front-row. In those days, rugby had replacements for injury but not substitutes. For a horrible moment it looked as if an international match would proceed with uncontested scrums. (The referee must order these when, for whatever reason, a team can't provide enough front-row players. There's no shoving, no contest for the ball, and the team putting it in must win it. Very tame stuff, which the Cardiff crowd would not have enjoyed.) The captains did some fast thinking, and agreed with the referee that another Welsh forward should also leave the field so that a 'substitute' front-row player could come on. This scenario is now enshrined in law.

How many on the bench?

For international matches, a Union can nominate up to seven players as replacements/substitutes. For all other matches, the Union with jurisdiction has responsibility for deciding how many may be nominated. Bearing in mind the Cardiff Scenario and the need to avoid uncontested scrums, the laws make certain conditions. A team that nominates 16, 17, or 18 players for a match must include at least four who can play in the front row. If the team nominates 19, 20, 21 or 22 players, at least five must be front-row players. And no matter how many get nominated, a team may substitute no more than two front-row players and no more than five in other positions.

How many in a team?

Here's a clue. The answer is not fifteen.

When replacement/substitution arrived in a big way, the lawmakers changed the definition of a 'team'. It now means the players out there on the field (maximum fifteen) plus all the replacements/substitutes waiting to take part. And the referee's authority covers *all* these players, whether they are on or off the park. If a replacement/substitute who is still in his tracksuit does anything that would be unacceptable on the field-of-play, the referee can penalise his team with a penalty kick on the 15-metre line. Or more. I've never heard of a replacement/substitute getting sent off before he even came on, but there's a first time for everything.

The slippery slope

Without replacement, a good game can be knocked sideways if a key player has to depart injured. In that respect, replacement is a good thing; but let nobody kid himself that it has not created new problems while it solved old ones. For a start it means having players who will probably not play and who will certainly not play the full match. Other sports – basketball, soccer, American football – stand as grim warnings of what can happen when replacement/substitution gets out of hand. Rugby has started to slide down that slippery slope.

Which raises a central question. Who's in charge? The lawmakers settled for the passive tense: *substitutes may be made.* That's fine on paper, but the game isn't played on paper; and nowhere in the lawbook does it define the role of the coach or manager or whoever it is who thinks it's time to pull off the scrum-half and send on a substitute. What gives him the right to interfere with play? Presumably the answer is: the agreement of the players. But what if the scrum-half thinks he's playing a blinder and refuses to leave? What then? Don't say it couldn't happen. In rugby, anything can happen, and I guarantee that this will happen, sooner or later.

'If there's no fun in it, there's no future in it'

I didn't say that; the All Black Chris Laidlaw said it. He was talking about rugby, and he was right. One reason the game has not only survived for over a hundred years but also spread and flourished throughout the world, is that underrated word, fun. Outsiders may find it hard to believe that hundreds of thousands of rugby players spend their Saturday afternoons bringing each other down with a sickening thud simply because they enjoy it, but it's a fact. The game is no longer entirely amateur, but that doesn't mean it's entirely professional. Rugby is now an open game, like golf or tennis. You can play it for money (if you're good enough), or you can play it just for the satisfaction of doing so – and that's what 99% of all players will go on doing. The spirit that fuels rugby is fun.

Appendix A: Under-19 variations

Like all laws, these come from the International Rugby Board. They apply world-wide to the 15-a-side game when played at Under-19 level (U19), meaning a player is under the age of 19.

Time: 35 minutes each way. Play in any U19 match must not last longer than 70 minutes. Even in a knock-out competition, extra time must not be played.

Replacement and substitution. This follows the same lines as in the laws governing the senior game, except that a player who has been substituted may replace an injured player. The number of replacements/substitutes is the responsibility of the Union with jurisdiction over the match.

Scrum

Not within 5 metres of a goal line. When the stoppage or infringement is less than 5 metres from a goal line, the scrum must be on the 5-metre line.

Front rows meeting. For safety's sake, each prop shall touch his opponent's upper arm and then pause before the front rows meet. The sequence should be: crouch, touch, pause, engage.

Wheeling. A team must not intentionally wheel a scrum. If an unintentional wheel passes 45 degrees, the referee orders another scrum. Penalty: Penalty kick.

Maximum shove: 1.5m. A team in a scrum must not shove it more than 1.5 metres forward. Penalty: Free kick.

Must release ball. Once a team has heeled the ball and they control it at the base, they must not keep it in the scrum. Penalty: Free kick.

Scrum formation must be 3-4-1, with the No. 8 packing between the two locks and binding on them. However, if a complete team is not available, or if a player gets sent off or goes off because of injury, a scrum can have fewer than eight players per team. When that happens, the scrum formations are as follows:

- If a team lacks one player, both teams must use a 3–4 formation (no No. 8).
- If a team lacks two players, both teams must use a 3–2–1 formation (no flankers).
- If a team lacks three players, both teams must use a 3–2 formation (front five only).

Even so, each team must always have at least five players in a scrum.

Uncontested scrums. If a team cannot field suitably trained players for any of the front five positions (prop, hooker, lock), the referee must order uncontested scrums. In these, there is no shoving, the teams do not compete for the ball, and the team putting it in must win it.

Dangerous play

'Flying Wedge' banned. This tactic is usually used when the attacking team is awarded a kick near the goal line. They take a tap-kick and drive forward in a wedge formation.

'Cavalry Charge' banned. This also usually develops from an attackers' tap-kick near the goal line. Attacking players form a line across the field, some distance behind the kicker. At a signal, they charge forward and one of them takes a pass.

Both the 'Flying Wedge' and the 'Cavalry Charge' are dangerous and illegal at all levels.

Appendix B: Seven-a-side variations

Made by the International Rugby Board to standardise play worldwide.

Maximum numbers. Each team has no more than seven players.

Three players from each team form a scrum. They must remain bound until it ends.

Replacement and substitution. This follows the same lines as the 15-a-side game. A team can nominate no more than three replacements/substitutes. Up to three players may be replaced or substituted. A player who has been substituted cannot return to that match except to replace a bleeding player.

Maximum time is 14 minutes, with a one-minute interval at half-time, except for the final of a competition, which lasts no longer than 20 minutes, with a two-minute interval. Play is divided into halves.

Extra time: sudden death. When a match is drawn and extra time is needed, the captains must toss a coin for the right to kick off or choose ends. Extra time is played in periods of five minutes. After each period, the teams change ends without an interval. The one that scores first is immediately declared the winner and the match ends.

Conversion kick must be a drop kick, which the kicker can take even if team-mates are still in front of him. As soon as a try is scored, the team scored against go immediately to the area of their own 10-metre line.

After a score, the scoring team re-starts, with a drop kick from the centre. If this fails to reach the 10-metre line (unless first touched by an opponent) or if it goes directly into touch, their opponents are awarded a free kick at the centre.

No place kicks, except to start the match and re-start it after half-time. Any penalty kick cannot be a place kick.

No delay. Everything the Laws say about the need to take kicks without delay applies especially to Seven-a-Side rugby. If the kicker is slow, the referee should warn him. If the delay is intentional, the referee can disallow the kick without warning.

In-goal judges. These act as extra touch judges, one in each goal area.

Apart from these variations, all the Laws of the Game apply.

Index